The Effective Induction of Newly Qualified Primary Teachers

An Induction Tutor's Handbook

Sara Bubb

David Fulton Publishers
London

David Fulton Publishers Ltd
The Chiswick Centre, 414 Chiswick High Road, London W4 5TF
www.fultonpublishers.co.uk

First published in Great Britain in 2000 by David Fulton Publishers

Note: The rights of Sara Bubb to be identified as the authors of this work have
been asserted by them in accordance with the Copyright, Designs and Patents
Act 1988.

David Fulton Publishers is a division of Granada Learning Limited, part of
Granada plc.

British Library Cataloguing in Publication Data
A catalogue record for this book is available from the British Library.

ISBN 1-85346-684-0

Typeset by Textype Typesetters, Cambridge
Printed and bound in Great Britain

Contents

Foreword

Induction into any profession is likely to be exacting. Making the transition from someone who studies a job to an effective practitioner requires knowledge to be turned into practical know-how, the development of high levels of social skills and the assimilation of the culture of the work place. As this new book illustrates, the processes of induction are particularly tricky in today's schools where colleagues with responsibility for supporting new entrants to the profession are also charged with judging their capabilities and monitoring their progress.

Sara Bubb has drawn on her experience as a teacher, a teacher-trainer and an inspector to analyse exactly what needs to be done in order to maximise the value of the induction process for new teachers and to guide the work of experienced tutors so that their role is both rigorous and gratifying. She has tested her understanding of induction by running courses for tutors and by interrogating the latest research findings on the subject. The result is a comprehensive handbook packed with information, a set of useful forms and a series of related activities with which induction tutors can test their own understanding of the most pertinent issues.

The teaching profession has come a long way since the early days of state education: all kinds of knowledge have vastly increased; far more pedagogical skills and techniques now exist; and the computer offers enormous potential benefits. At the same time, pupils are more knowledgable about most aspects of life and more confident about challenging accepted school practice. Such changes will continue and are likely to increase, still further, the pressures on teachers.

If the educators of the future are expected to reach higher standards of teaching, induction tutors will need to ensure that they have the best professional start to their career. Sara Bubb's book offers a way to make this possible. I commend it with enthusiasm.

Peter Mortimore
Institute of Education
University of London
May 2000

Preface

Teaching children is a very rewarding job, albeit demanding. Teaching newly qualified teachers (NQTs) – for that is what induction tutors do – can be even more rewarding because the effects of an induction programme will last throughout a teacher's career, having an impact on hundreds or thousands of children.

Being an induction tutor is not the same as being a mentor – a term that means different things to different people. An induction tutor is more than a wise and trusted adviser. Even people who are experienced mentors of students and NQTs have found the new role difficult, because induction tutors are responsible for three areas: support, monitoring and assessment (DfEE 1999, p. 2). Most people feel happy in the support role, but find that their responsibilities for monitoring and assessment can conflict with this. As one induction tutor said:

> I can be supportive but I also have to withdraw at times, and be quite formal. I felt uncomfortable in the assessor role at first, but training has helped.

Many induction tutors also feel worried about how well they are carrying out their role. They do not know whether they are expecting too much or too little of their NQTs. Some even welcome an OFSTED inspection because it gives them an objective measure of how well their NQTs are teaching.

Being an induction tutor is difficult for other reasons:

– the responsibilities are huge and not fully understood;
– there is no funding earmarked for induction tutors;
– few schools allocate time for induction tutors to do their work;
– the role carries little status in many schools;
– induction tutors get little advice or training in the role; and
– some NQTs require much more help than others.

My aim in writing this book is to make the induction tutor's life easier by providing clear explanations and useful formats for recording their work. I hope to help them through the induction period: from the initial visit, to analysing the Career Entry Profile (CEP), to understanding the Standards, to setting objectives, to judging progress and, finally, to completing assessment reports. There are some key publications that induction tutors need and to which this book makes reference. These are Circular 5/99 *The Induction Period for Newly Qualified Teachers* (telephone 0845 602 2260 for a copy), the TTA *Career Entry Profile*, and the TTA *Supporting Induction* booklets (telephone 0845 606 0323 for copies).

Sara Bubb
April 2000

Acknowledgements

This book has been written as a practical guide for induction tutors to help them support the professional development of newly qualified teachers (NQTs). As such, I would like to thank all the people who come to my courses at the University of London Institute of Education and at the Lewisham and Lambeth Professional Development Centres. These groups of NQTs and induction tutors have been an inspiration and guide to me in writing what I hope is a very practical book.

My past and present PGCE students at the Institute must also be acknowledged, because they have given me such insights into how people learn to be teachers. I hope this book will help them get a fair deal in their first year of teaching.

I have made every effort to acknowledge sources throughout the book and would particularly like to thank the induction team at the TTA who have been a valuable resource.

Most of all, I must thank Paul, Julian, Miranda and Oliver for their encouragement and tolerance while I wrote this book.

1 The statutory induction arrangements

Background

The induction of newly qualified teachers has been an issue for many years. In 1972 the James Report on *Teacher Education and Training* highlighted the importance of a structured programme of induction for new teachers. HMI (1988) found that the quality of provision for NQTs was highly variable. They found that secondary schools were more likely to be able to support new teachers than primary schools, but that neither built well on initial teacher training. There was a feeling that one could forget what had been learned in college once the real job of teaching began. HMI also felt that the assessment of teachers was often impressionistic, and based too rarely on evidence. Significantly, they found that a high proportion of weak teachers had had poor induction.

Before September 1999 many NQTs did not have:

- a permanent contract
- release time
- the chance to go on LEA induction programmes
- the opportunity to observe other teachers
- feedback on how they were doing
- someone to observe them
- a mentor with time for the job
- a mentor trained in the skills for the job
- account taken of their training and previous experience.

In 1992 the probationary year was abolished. Between then and the arrangements for a statutory induction period for newly qualified teachers which started in September 1999, there was no requirement for schools to provide induction. As Kevan Bleach says,

> There was little more than the professional integrity of heads, teachers and advisers to sustain and encourage good practice. (1999b, p.12)

NQTs experienced even more variable support during these seven years, than when the probationary year was in place. Some LEAs continued with an extensive induction programme and training for mentors, but many found this hard to maintain. Some schools supported and monitored NQTs well but others treated them as cannon fodder, giving only short-term contracts and no help. Figure 1.1 shows a group of NQTs' feelings about the support they had during their first year of teaching. The survey was conducted at the end of the 1998–99 academic year, just before induction was made statutory. The teachers were from primary schools in an inner London borough which had run a successful induction and mentoring programme. The variability even within a small geographical area is striking. The quarter of respondents who did not feel supported in their induction year wrote passionately about what had gone wrong, or rather what had not happened at all.

Before Circular 5/99, the only way that schools could get rid of ineffective teachers was to go through lengthy competency procedures. This led many to give temporary contracts, usually for one year, but sometimes for one term or less. This was clearly unsatisfactory for all concerned. People without permanent contracts found it very difficult to get loans or mortgages, and justifiably questioned the point of giving one hundred per cent to a school which they might only be in for a short time.

How helpful was the induction support in your school?				
Awful	Unsatisfactory	Satisfactory	Good	Very Good
12%	13%	38%	16%	21%

Positive comments

Excellent support from mentor and all other members of staff, including non-teaching staff.

It's important to have formal provision in school and I found it helpful.

Mentor always available for advice. Staff very supportive. Non-contact time every week.

All staff, including my mentor, have been supportive but within the constraints of their own teaching commitments.

Excellent support especially from year group partner, mentor, head, deputy, SENCO.

Negative comments

Schools need to support new teachers more. If they can't, they shouldn't employ them. The only support I got was being allowed to come on the LEA induction course.

I had to actively seek help, otherwise I wouldn't have got any. Had a mentor in theory, but in practice any support was on a casual 'friendship' basis.

Mentor chosen half a term after I began and she's only in her second year of teaching, didn't train in the UK, and hasn't got experience of teaching in my phase. The head never visits classrooms so there was no verbal or practical support from her. I still haven't been shown around the school! Policies are vague, schemes of work are vaguer!

The school claimed it had little money for NQT support so I didn't get much. I was just expected to get on with it.

I think I had a mentor, but I'm not actually sure. I think I missed out because I started in the school as a supply teacher and then got a temporary contract.

School is in special measures and priorities are elsewhere, not on us. The pressure has been immense and support totally inadequate.

Figure 1.1 NQTs' feelings about their school induction programme, July 1999

The DfEE Circular

In May 1999, the DfEE published Circular 5/99 *The Induction Period for Newly Qualified Teachers*. This described induction as 'a bridge from initial teacher training to effective professional practice' (para. 1). The expectation was that supporting people well at the start of their career would 'help them to give of their best to pupils and to make a real and sustained contribution to school improvement and to raising classroom Standards' (para. 1).

The circular put into place a hurdle to be crossed before complete entry into the profession is guaranteed. The Association of Teachers and Lecturers (ATL) (1999) sums up the different interpretations of this in the title of its publication *Induction: Bridge or Barrier?* NQTs have to meet demanding Standards at the end of the induction period before being allowed to continue to teach.

> NQTs must demonstrate that they have continued to meet the Standards for the award of QTS on a consistent basis in an employment context and met all the Induction Standards to satisfactorily complete the induction period. (DfEE 1999, para. 5)

How is induction funded?

At the time of writing, maintained schools are given money for induction through Grant 1 of the Standards Fund. The TTA says

> The assumption is that LEAs will identify and delegate to their schools funds that are at least sufficient to secure the 10% reduction in NQTs' timetables and to cover the costs of training for inductees, line managers, head teachers and mentors. (TTA 1999b, p. 31)

However, Grant 1 is for many other school improvement initiatives. The whole amount is devolved by LEAs in the way that they see fit – 'there will inevitably be winners and losers' as one official said. This means, in practice, that some schools have barely enough to cover the NQT's 10 per cent release time, let alone money to send induction tutors and NQTs on courses. I have met many NQTs who have suffered because of confusion over funding. They have, for instance, not had a reduced timetable until the second term.

Who must complete the statutory induction period?

People who were awarded Qualified Teacher Status (QTS) after 7 May 1999 have had to complete an induction period of a school year (or equivalent) if they are to work in maintained primary or secondary schools, or in non-maintained special schools in England. Those who qualified before May 1999 do not have to go through statutory induction, even if they do not take up their first post until after September 1999.

NQTs who are awarded QTS, but who do not satisfactorily complete a statutory induction period, will *not* be eligible for employment as a teacher in a maintained school or non-maintained special school. However, their QTS cannot be taken away from them.

Only teachers with QTS are entitled to induction. Those who have teaching qualifications outside the European Union have to gain QTS in England through, for instance, the Graduate Teacher Scheme.

Teachers do not, by law, have to complete an induction year if they work in the independent sector, though they would need to if they moved to the state sector. However, they can complete their induction period in an independent school if it teaches the National Curriculum. The Independent Schools Council recommends that their members provide induction.

Supply teachers can only start their induction period if they are employed for a full term to teach the same class. NQTs can only work as supply teachers for four terms after their first appointment, before taking a settled job in which to do their induction period. This should benefit teachers because they will get the support and further training that they need.

Where can NQTs complete their induction period?

Schools which can provide an induction period are:

(a) maintained schools;
(b) non-maintained special schools;
(c) independent primary schools, if they teach National Curriculum Key Stages 1 and 2.

Schools that cannot provide induction include:

(a) pupil referral units;
(b) schools requiring special measures unless one of Her Majesty's Inspectors certifies in writing that the school is suitable for providing induction;
(c) independent schools that do not teach the National Curriculum.

At the time of writing, teachers are not allowed to complete their induction year abroad, even if they are working in British schools. This is because there is no Appropriate Body for these schools.

The Appropriate Body

The school needs to have an Appropriate Body to which they send reports and which has a quality assurance role. All LEAs act as Appropriate Bodies. In independent schools, the appropriate body will be either the LEA for the area in which the school is situated or the Independent Schools Council Teacher Induction Panel (ISCTIP).

The Appropriate Body has two key responsibilities:

- to assure itself that schools understand, and are able to meet, their responsibilities for monitoring, support and guidance and for undertaking a rigorous and equitable assessment of the NQT; and
- to decide, in the light of the head teacher's recommendation, whether an NQT has satisfactorily completed the induction period, and to communicate this decision to the NQT, the head teacher, the General Teaching Council (GTC), and the DfEE. It may, in exceptional circumstances, offer an NQT the opportunity of an extension to the induction period. (Circular Annex C, 15–21) (TTA 1999b, p.113)

It must also identify a named contact on induction matters, with whom NQTs may raise issues about their induction programme where they cannot be resolved satisfactorily within the school.

The components of the induction period

Circular 5/99 states that

> The induction period will combine an individualised programme of monitoring and support, which provides opportunities for NQTs to develop further their knowledge, skills and achievements in relation to the Standards for the award of QTS, with an assessment of their performance. (DfEE 1999, para. 4)

The key words are *monitoring, support, assessment.*

In practice this means that there is an entitlement for NQTs that should last throughout their induction period. This is three terms or the equivalent. Thus if an NQT only works two and a half days a week their induction period will last for six terms.

NQTs are entitled to the following:

1. A job description that does not make unreasonable demands (see below).
2. An induction tutor.
3. Meetings with the induction tutor.
4. The Career Entry Profile (CEP) discussed by NQT and induction tutor.
5. Objectives, informed by the strengths and areas for development identified in the CEP, to help NQTs improve so that they meet the Standards for the induction period.
6. A 10 per cent reduction in timetable – this will be half a day off a week or the equivalent.
7. A planned programme of how to spend that time, such as observing other teachers.
8. At least one observation each half term with oral and written feedback, meaning a total of at least six a year.
9. An assessment meeting towards the end of each term.
10. An assessment report at the end of each term. This will usually be written by the induction tutor, but has a box for the NQT's comments.
11. Procedures for NQTs to air grievances about their induction provision at school and a 'named person' to contact at the appropriate body, usually the LEA.

Circular 5/99 says that teachers in their induction year should not be given a job description that makes unreasonable demands. This should apply equally to those working on a part-time or long-term supply basis. Specifically, an NQT should normally serve the induction period in a post which:

– does not demand teaching outside the age range and subject(s) for which the NQT has been trained;
– does not present the NQT on a day-to-day basis with acute or especially demanding discipline problems;
– involves regular teaching of the same class(es);
– involves similar planning, teaching and assessment processes to those in which teachers working in substantive posts in the school are engaged; and
– does not involve additional non-teaching responsibilities without the provision of appropriate preparation and support. (DfEE 1999, para. 26)

Roles and responsibilities

It is essential that everyone is clear about their role and responsibilities. The TTA outlines the roles clearly in the booklet *Supporting Induction for Newly Qualified Teachers Part 1: Overview*, from which the following are taken.

The newly qualified teacher
NQTs should take an active role in all aspects of the induction process. They should:

● make their Career Entry Profile available to the school, and work with their induction tutor to use the Career Entry Profile and the Induction Standards as a basis for setting objectives for professional development and devising an action plan;

- take part in planning their induction programme, including the identification and reviewing of objectives;
- engage fully in the programme of monitoring, support and assessment that is agreed with the induction tutor, taking increasing responsibility for their professional development as the induction period progresses;
- be familiar with the Induction Standards, monitor their own work in relation to them and contribute to the collection of evidence towards their formal assessment;
- raise any concerns they have about the content and/or delivery of their induction programme.

The head teacher

The head teacher has two key responsibilities:

- to ensure that each NQT in their school is provided with an appropriate induction programme, in line with national arrangements; and
- to make a recommendation to the LEA, based on rigorous and fair assessment procedures, as to whether the NQT has met the Induction Standards.

In order to meet these responsibilities, the head teacher should:

- designate an induction tutor for each NQT, and ensure that this person is adequately prepared and is able to work effectively in the role. In some cases, the head teacher may wish to designate themselves as an induction tutor;
- ensure that any duties assigned to the NQT are reasonable;
- ensure that the NQT is provided with a timetable representing no more than 90 per cent of the average contact time normally allocated to more experienced teachers in the school, and ensure that the time released is protected, is distributed appropriately throughout the induction period and is used to support the NQT's professional development right from the start of the induction period;
- provide the NQT with a way of raising concerns about the induction programme, and make sure that these concerns are addressed satisfactorily;
- inform the LEA about any NQT who may be at risk of failing to meet the Induction Standards and observe the teaching of any NQT concerned;
- keep the Governing Body informed about arrangements for the induction of NQTs in the school, and the results of formal assessment meetings.

Tasks which the head teacher may wish to delegate, while retaining overall responsibility, are:

- devising, together with the NQT, a targeted and appropriate monitoring, support and assessment programme, building on the Career Entry Profile and drawing on external resources where relevant;
- making arrangements for any additional experience that the NQT may need to gain in settings outside the school, for example in a nursery setting, or for further support that needs to be provided by specialists for an NQT teaching a minority subject;
- telling the LEA when any teacher who is subject to the induction arrangements either joins or leaves the school;
- sending the LEA the reports completed after formal assessment meetings;
- liaising with other head teachers and LEAs as appropriate in relation to NQTs employed on a part-time basis in more than one school at the same time;

- making sure that any relevant reports and records are obtained from any school(s) in which an NQT has served part of their induction, and forwarding copies of any previously completed assessment reports to the LEA;
- making sure that copies of all reports of observations, review meetings and objectives are kept until the induction period has been completed satisfactorily and any appeal determined;
- keeping copies of any records or assessment reports for those NQTs who leave the school before completing the induction period, and forwarding these to the NQT's new school when requested;
- submitting the relevant assessment form to the Appropriate Body within ten working days of completion of the induction period.

The induction tutor

The induction tutor has the day-to-day responsibility for the monitoring, support and assessment of a particular NQT. In many primary schools the induction tutor will be the deputy head teacher or a phase coordinator. The most important consideration is that the role is taken by an appropriately experienced colleague who has regular contact with the NQT.

The induction tutor needs to be fully aware of the requirements of the induction period and to have the skills, expertise and knowledge to work effectively in the role. In particular, they should be able to provide or coordinate effective guidance and support, and to make rigorous and fair judgements about the new teacher's performance in relation to the Induction Standards.

As well as any tasks delegated by the head teacher, the responsibilities of the induction tutor include:

- making sure the NQT knows and understands the roles and responsibilities of those involved in induction, including their own rights and their responsibility to take an active role in their own professional development;
- organising and implementing, in consultation with the NQT, a tailored programme of monitoring, support and assessment (see Circular, paragraphs 40–54) that takes forward in a flexible way the action plan set out in the NQT's Career Entry Profile and which takes into account the needs and strengths identified in the Profile, the Induction Standards, and the specific context of the school;
- coordinating or carrying out observations of the NQT's teaching and organising follow-up discussions with the NQT;
- reviewing with the NQT their progress against their objectives and the Induction Standards;
- making sure that the NQT is fully informed about the nature and purpose of assessment in the induction period;
- ensuring that dated records are kept of monitoring, support and formative and summative assessment activities undertaken, and their outcomes.

As you can see, the induction tutor's role and responsibilites are huge. The next chapter goes into more detail about this role and how to make it manageable and effective.

2 Being an induction tutor

Research into effective teaching (e.g. Eraut 1994, Woods and Jeffreys 1996) indicates that teachers need help in becoming 'reflective and proactive practitioners' from modelling themselves on competent colleagues (Moyles *et al.* 1999). This is the role that induction tutors take. It is a huge responsibility, but there are enormous gains to be made. Firstly, the NQT develops into a more effective teacher. The role also results in greater understanding of both self-as-teacher and self-as-induction tutor (Moyles *et al.*) and improved performance in both roles.

Teachers are chosen to be induction tutors for a variety of reasons, but always because the head teacher thinks they will do the job well. Such recognition is very flattering. Here are what some teachers at the start of the statutory induction year wrote in response to the question: How do you feel about being an induction tutor?

'Enjoyable part of working life – rewarding, challenging, though frustrating at times.'

'I am quite happy – feel it is both challenging and interesting.'

'A compliment!'

'Very pleased – I think it is an important role, and also a satisfying one.'

'Generally confident, though a little concerned as to how this year will go (with lots of NQTs on board).'

'Excited and aware of the enormous responsibility. Determined to do it well.'

'I welcome the opportunity to guide and learn from the NQT.'

'Brilliant – makes us "old uns" feel optimistic for the future.'

'I thoroughly enjoy this important aspect of my work.'

'Apprehensive. It is a huge responsibility – terrifying.'

Working with adults

Induction tutors are chosen because, amongst other things, they are good teachers. But good teachers of children may not necessarily be good teachers of adults. Many of the skills of teaching children, however, can be transferred to working with adults. Here are some similarities and differences that it would be useful to consider.

What is different about teaching adults, rather than children?

The relationship between adults is more equal. On the surface, most adults seem 'equal' but in practice all manner of power games may come into play. Usually NQTs will feel inferior. However, many will have more academic qualifications than other staff. A great many will have more up-to-date theoretical knowledge because they will have had to cover the demanding Initial Teacher Training National Curricula for English, mathematics, science and ICT. Some will be older than their induction tutor.

Although the induction tutor will be a more experienced (though sometimes not much more) teacher, they may not ultimately be better at helping children learn. It can be very uncomfortable, humbling and potentially threatening when you are being the tutor for someone at the start of their career who is already a better teacher than you will ever be. I speak from experience. It can also be extremely exciting, and cause one to improve one's own teaching. Many induction tutors speak of how they benefit from helping NQTs, not only because they reflect on their own practice but because they gain new insights and ideas.

Instead of a class of 30, the induction tutor normally only works with one or two new teachers. This leads to more friendship and intimacy. This is usually a bonus, but can lead to the relationship becoming intense. Some NQTs can become over-reliant on their induction tutor. Strong friendships develop, which might inhibit the induction tutor from pointing out areas for development in an objective way.

Clearly you cannot be bossy with adults. Tempting as it may seem, you cannot really tell them off, reward them with a sticker or punish them with a missed playtime. Sometimes you have to skirt around issues, hoping that hints will be enough. Most adults behave well, understand what you are saying and respond well to advice. Some, however, have special needs and may require the same thing said in several different ways!

Adults have a great deal of 'baggage' compared with children. Most NQTs have enormously high expectations of themselves and can quickly lose self-confidence when things do not go right. They will often have been fairly successful in teaching practice if not throughout life, and feel stunned when they cannot manage all the children in the class. Some will have had damaging experiences at school that will call for sensitivity when commenting on spelling mistakes, for instance.

Adults, like children, have home lives that may be less than ideal. Almost all NQTs will join the profession in quite serious financial debt because of having to borrow money while at university. It is easy for established teachers to forget that, though not rich, they are more comfortably off than most NQTs. Many will be living in poor shared accommodation, have little money for transport, food, clothes and extras. Some have appallingly long and difficult journeys on public transport that significantly increase the length and stress of their working day. Inevitably NQTs' personal relationships become strained, especially when they are too drained from a day's teaching to respond to loved ones and see friends.

Lessons to learn from working successfully with children

1. If we think about the way we like to be treated as adults and how children learn best, we will be better induction tutors.

2. See your role as someone who allows the NQT to reflect off and who asks the questions that encourage them to think of the solutions themselves. A quotation that I find immensely powerful is:

> A leader is best
> When people barely know he exists,
> Not so good when people obey him and acclaim him,
> Worst when they despise him.
> But of a good leader, who talks little,
> When his work is done, his aim fulfilled,
> They will all say 'We did this ourselves'.

Lao-Tse

3. Aim to be person-centred in the same way that as teachers we are child-centred. Think of the NQT's needs and interests. This, of course, must be married with the need to conform to the Induction Standards and school philosophy, in the same way as children have to work within the National Curriculum.
4. Be sensitive to their beliefs and educational philosophy. There are many ways to teach children. They may not teach like you do, but that doesn't mean you are right – the proof is in the progress that the children make.
5. Children and adults alike thrive on praise. Accentuate the positive and people will be more open to hearing the negative. Say something nice and the world turns more smoothly.
6. People think of their own solutions to problems if they are given structures such as focused time to think about the issue and someone to ask guiding open-ended questions and discuss with.
7. No one learns well when they are tired, hungry, ill or stressed. Make sure that all staff keep an eye on the NQT.
8. Make instructions and expectations clear. In a school people sometimes give different messages and contradictory advice. This clearly is not helpful.
9. Like children, adults learn by being shown and having the opportunity to see others doing it right.
10. People thrive when they are treated with respect. They do not make progress when intimidated or when they feel a failure.

The roles of an induction tutor

The induction tutor is the person with specific responsibility for an NQT. It is a really important role and one which is very rewarding. Some teachers have said that it is the favourite of all their roles in school. One way of thinking about the sort of induction tutor you would like to be is to analyse what it was that the people who have helped you be a better teacher did or said (see Activity 2.1). The significant colleagues in my career engaged with me at a high level in thinking about education. They were people who held the same educational philosophy as me, and had the same values. We shared many interests and a sense of humour. They believed in me – and that gave me confidence to try new things.

Activity 2.1
Remembering someone who helped you be a better teacher

Think of a colleague who made a difference to you; someone who inspired you, kept you going, etc.

List some of their characteristics or actions that helped you become a better teacher.

Roles that an NQT might need people to take

It is useful to think of the different sorts of roles an NQT might want from people in their first year in a primary school. These might include:

Planning partner	Critical friend
Disciplinarian of the NQT's pupils	Facilitator
Monitor of progress	Expert practitioner
Colleague	Organiser
Friend	Trainer
Supporter	Protector
Adviser	Assessor
Counsellor	Motivator
Helper	Parent

Clearly the induction tutor could not and should not take on all these roles. The whole staff is responsible for inducting a new teacher, and different people will take on certain roles naturally. In my first year of teaching a classroom assistant played a big role in looking after me by doing lots of little things like bringing me coffee and generally being like a mum. Not all NQTs need someone on the staff to fulfil all these roles, perhaps because they are confident and highly skilled already or because there are other people in their lives who have these roles. Remember, however, that some NQTs are very isolated, living on their own in a new area.

Problems may arise when key roles are not taken by someone in the NQT's life. Equally problematic is when one person takes on too many roles. This can easily happen to induction tutors because they feel responsible for the NQT. Activity 2.2 contains a useful exercise to think about or discuss with the NQT concerning who takes on the different roles they need.

Activity 2.2
Roles that might be needed by an NQT

1. Tick the roles you have engaged in so far as an induction tutor.
2. Write the names of other staff who take any of these roles. Some may be taken by several people.
3. Does your NQT agree?
4. Are any roles not covered?
5. Do you feel happy with the balance of roles?

Planning partner ☐ _____ _____ _____

Disciplinarian of the
NQT's pupils ☐ _____ _____ _____

Monitor of progress ☐ _____ _____ _____

Colleague ☐ _____ _____ _____

Friend ☐ _____ _____ _____

Supporter ☐ _____ _____ _____

Adviser ☐ _____ _____ _____

Counsellor ☐ _____ _____ _____

Helper ☐ _____ _____ _____

Critical friend ☐ _____ _____ _____

Facilitator ☐ _____ _____ _____

Expert practitioner ☐ _____ _____ _____

Organiser ☐ _____ _____ _____

Trainer ☐ _____ _____ _____

Protector ☐ _____ _____ _____

Assessor ☐ _____ _____ _____

Motivator ☐ _____ _____ _____

Parent ☐ _____ _____ _____

Being aware of the stages that NQTs go through

There is a common perception that a person should be able to teach well having been awarded QTS. Certainly, the children in their class have a right to a good education. However, experienced teachers know that it is a job that can never be done perfectly – one can always improve. The more I know about teaching and learning the more I realise there is to know. This is what makes it such a great job – but also such a potentially depressing one.

There is a huge difference between novice and experienced teachers. Like any skill or craft, learning to teach is a developmental process characterised by devastating disasters and spectacular successes. How NQTs feel about their job changes on a daily basis at first. One day will be great and leave the NQT feeling positive and idealistic, but the next will be diabolical and they will dread walking back through the school gates. As time goes on most find that good days outnumber the bad ones, and they realise they are actually enjoying their job. So, NQTs need different levels and types of support at different times during their first year. Bullough (1989) describes in detail the stages that one new teacher went through. I have used Maynard and Furlong's (1993) five stages of development that trainee teachers go through, to illustrate their development over the induction year (see Figure 2.1).

Stages that new teachers experience	
Early idealism	Feeling that everything is possible and having a strong picture of how they want to teach: 'I'll never shout at a child'. Bullough refers to this as the 'fantasy' stage where teachers imagine children hanging on their every word.
Survival	The NQT lives from day to day, needing quick fixes and tips. They find it hard to solve problems because there are so many of them. Behaviour management is of particular concern – they have nightmares about losing control. They are too stressed and busy to reflect. Colds and sore throats plague them. Survival often characterises the first term, especially in the run-up to Christmas.
Recognising difficulties	They can see problems more clearly. They can identify difficulties and think of solutions because there is some space in their lives. They move forward. This stage is aided considerably by a skilled induction tutor.
Hitting the plateau	Key problems, such as behaviour management and organisation, have been solved so they feel things are going well. They feel they are mastering teaching. They begin to enjoy it and do not find it too hard. But, they do not want to tackle anything different, or take on any radical new initiatives. If forced they will pay lip-service to new developments. Some teachers spend the rest of their career at this stage.
Moving on	They are ready for further challenges. They want to try out different styles of teaching, new age groups, coordinate a subject. If their present school does not offer them sufficient challenge they will apply for a new job.

Figure 2.1 Five stages that NQTs go through (based on Maynard and Furlong 1993, pp. 12–13)

The usefulness of the model in Figure 2.1 is that induction teachers can plan and adapt their input, depending on the stage of their NQT. For instance, there is no point in expecting the NQT to think deeply about assessment when they are in the Survival stage, battling with control. Equally, they will not want quick tips if they are at the Moving on stage.

What NQTs want from an induction tutor

When one asks NQTs what they value most about their induction tutors they are very clear. They are even more clear about where they do not feel well supported by the school (see Figure 1.1). Here is what a large group of NQTs said about their induction tutors.

Characteristics of effective induction tutors – NQTs' views
1. They were always available for advice.
2. They gave me a regular meeting time, even though they were busy.
3. They were genuinely interested in how I was doing.
4. They were honest and open, which encouraged trust.
5. They listened to me – and didn't impose their own views.
6. They made practical suggestions.
7. They shared their expertise, ideas and resources.
8. They were encouraging and optimistic – they made me feel good.
9. They stopped me working myself into the ground by setting realistic objectives.
10. They weren't perfect themselves, which was reassuring!
11. They looked after me, keeping parents and the Head off my back.
12. Their feedback after observations was useful. Good to get some praise and ideas for improvements.
13. It helped when they wrote the end of term reports because these gave us a clear picture of how we were doing.
14. They were well organised, and if they said they'd do something they did it.

More than anything, NQTs value someone who can give them time. This is a very precious resource in a primary school. Induction tutors often have many other very time-consuming roles and their time spent on induction is often not funded. The DfEE has rightly devoted money to ensuring that NQTs have a 10 per cent reduced timetable, but there is little extra to cover the potentially enormous costs of paying the people who are doing the support, monitoring and assessment. As ever, much has to be done on goodwill.

Head teachers often ask people to be induction tutors without realising what is involved, which is a great deal now that induction is statutory. Induction tutors need to shout to be heard.

What induction tutors can do to make the job manageable

Being an induction tutor is a huge role but it can be made manageable, not least by ensuring that people recognise the importance and nature of the job. Here are some suggestions.

1. Get 'induction tutor' written into your job description – and ideally delegate some other area of responsibility. Alternatively arrange with your head teacher to put one of your other responsibilities on the back burner, at least for the NQT's first term.
2. Arrange to receive training, and obtain resources (such as this book!) for the role. The ATL research recommends that 'NQTs should be entitled to support from a trained, rather than simply a named mentor' (Williams and Prestage 2000, p. 3). Most LEAs and universities run extensive induction training for NQTs, but the provision for those supporting them in schools is often limited to a couple of sessions. Shop around to find a course that gives you the level of training that you require. Some courses offer accreditation, which can be used towards an Advanced Diploma in Professional Studies or an MA. There are also whole MA modules in mentoring. This is a fairly painless way of getting something in return for all your hard work.
3. Be clear about your role and then be very organised. Set dates for meetings, assessment meetings and reports. Use the diary sheets in Figure 7.8 to help you map out the year. Make contacts with other schools so that you can arrange for your NQT to visit. See what topics are covered by NQT induction programmes organised by LEAs or universities. This will save you covering them yourself.
4. Have a fixed time for induction that everyone knows about, ideally during the school day. If it is after school, make sure that that time is sacrosanct and cannot be used for other meetings.
5. Book observation times and meetings into the school diary and make sure that they feature on weekly or half-termly sheets of events.
6. Buy the services of someone from outside the school to help with observations. This is useful if you feel that you do not have the time or expertise to make observations on the NQT, or if they are having problems. They will be able to give an objective picture of how your NQT is doing compared to others. Training institutions and LEAs might be able to recommend someone who is used to working with beginning teachers.
7. Develop your role by becoming the person responsible for students on teaching practice in your school. You will find this interesting and it will give you insights into the whole world of teacher education as you see people at different stages of courses. The skills of working with students are similar, though not the same, as those you use with NQTs.
8. Delegate parts of your role to others. For instance, plan for the head teacher and deputy to do some observations. Find someone to be the NQT's 'buddy mentor' and someone else to help them with planning and assessment. Remember that the whole school is responsible for induction.
9. Apply to be an Advanced Skills Teacher (DfEE 1998c). This is the new grade of teacher who is classroom based but who is required to participate in the induction of newly qualified teachers, among other things.

10. Cheer yourself up by reflecting on all that you have learnt from being an induction tutor. You are bound to have become a better teacher and manager from helping a novice, and probably feel hugely knowledgeable and experienced next to them. This is very boosting!

Keeping an induction tutor's file – how to keep evidence

It is important to keep a file of all that you do as an induction tutor because you will be accountable. You will need evidence to support your judgements, especially if there is debate about how well the NQT is doing. Think of the worst case scenario where an NQT does not pass the Induction Standards at the end of the year. They might say that they had insufficient help from their induction tutor. Outside bodies, such as the Appropriate Body and OFSTED, will also want to see how you have been monitoring, supporting and assessing the NQT.

NQTs should also keep evidence to demonstrate that they are meeting the Standards, using a format such as Figure 2.2. (This could be photocopied onto A3 paper, to allow further evidence, perhaps in each of the three terms.) However, the induction tutor should keep their own folder just in case the NQT loses documents such as lesson observation feedback sheets. Figures 2.3 and 2.4 have lists of what the induction tutor's and NQT's folders might contain.

In the next chapter we shall look at the Induction Standards. Although these are problematic, they are useful to induction tutors because they are fixed criteria by which to judge all NQTs.

Induction Standards	Progress
(a) Sets clear targets for improvement of pupils' achievement, monitors pupils' progress towards those targets and uses appropriate teaching strategies in the light of this, including, where appropriate, in relation to literacy, numeracy and other school targets.	
(b) Plans effectively to ensure that pupils have the opportunity to meet their potential, notwithstanding differences of race and gender, and taking account of the needs of pupils who are: ● underachieving; ● very able; ● not yet fluent in English; making use of relevant information and specialist help where available	
(c) Secures a good standard of pupil behaviour in the classroom through establishing appropriate rules and high expectations of discipline which pupils respect, acting to pre-empt and deal with inappropriate behaviour in the context of the behaviour policy of the school.	
(d) Plans effectively, where applicable, to meet the needs of pupils with Special Educational Needs and, in collaboration with the SENCO, makes an appropriate contribution to the preparation, implementation, monitoring and review of Individual Education Plans.	
(e) Takes account of ethnic and cultural diversity to enrich the curriculum and raise achievement.	
(f) Recognises the level that a pupil is achieving and makes accurate assessments, independently, against attainment targets, where applicable, and performance levels associated with other tests or qualifications relevant to the subject(s) or phase(s) taught.	
(g) Liaises effectively with pupils' parents/carers through informative oral and written reports on pupils' progress and achievements, discussing appropriate targets, and encouraging them to support their children's learning, behaviour and progress.	
(h) Where applicable, deploys support staff and other adults effectively in the classroom, involving them, where appropriate, in the planning and management of pupils learning.	
(i) Takes responsibility for implementing school policies and practices, including those dealing with bullying and racial harassment.	
(j) Takes responsibility for their own professional development, setting objectives for improvements, and taking action to keep up to date with research and developments in pedagogy and in the subjects they teach.	

Figure 2.2 NQT's record of progress in meeting the Induction Standards (TTA Career Entry Profile)

---

1. The school induction policy.
2. A copy of the NQT's Career Entry Profile.
3. Objectives and action plan (see Figures 4.3 and 5.4).
4. Diary sheets for the school-based induction programme (see Figure 7.4).
5. The NQT's record of training attended in and out of school (see Figure 7.3).
6. NQT's reflections on induction activities (see Figure 7.5).
7. Record sheets of induction meetings (see Figure 7.6).
8. Monitoring of planning and assessment (see Figures 8.2 and 8.3).
9. Monitoring of children's work (see Figure 8.4).
10. Observation and feedback on the NQT, by all observers (see Figures 8.5–8.8).
11. The NQT's termly self-evaluations (see Figure 9.2).
12. The NQT's record of progress in meeting the Standards (see Figure 2.2).
13. Agenda for termly assessment meetings (see Figure 9.1).
14. The termly reports on the NQT (see Appendix 2).
15. Documentation from the TTA and Appropriate Body (e.g. DfEE Circular 5/99, TTA Supporting Induction booklets).
16. Materials from induction tutor courses attended or articles read.

Figure 2.3 The contents of an induction tutor's file

---

1. The school induction policy.
2. The NQT's Career Entry Profile.
3. Objectives and action plan (see Figures 4.3 and 5.4).
4. Diary sheets for the school-based induction programme (see Figure 7.4).
5. A record of training attended in and out of school (see Figure 7.3).
6. Reflections on induction activities (see Figure 7.5).
7. Record sheets of induction meetings (see Figure 7.6).
8. Feedback on planning and assessment (see Figures 8.2 and 8.3) and children's work (see Figure 8.4).
9. Feedback on the NQT, by all observers (see Figures 8.5–8.8).
10. The NQT's termly self-evaluations (see Figure 9.2).
11. The NQT's record of progress in meeting the Standards (see Figure 2.2).
12. Agenda for termly assessment meetings (see Figure 9.1).
13. The termly assessment reports (see Appendix 2).
14. Documentation from the TTA and Appropriate Body (e.g. DFEE Circular 5/99, TTA Supporting Induction booklets).
15. Materials from courses attended or articles read.

Figure 2.4 The contents of an NQT's file

3 The Induction Standards

The Standards to be met

DfEE Circular 5/99 set in place the requirements for the induction year. These are twofold:

1. By the end of the induction period NQTs should have continued to meet the Standards for the award of Qualified Teacher Status consistently.
2. They should also have met all the Induction Standards.

The Standards for Qualified Teacher Status

We shall first consider the QTS Standards (DfEE 1998a). There are about 77 standards and sub-standards for students wanting to be primary teachers, and an additional 15 for those qualifying to teach reception and nursery classes. In the initial teacher training national curricula for English, mathematics, science and ICT there are hundreds of further standards. The QTS Standards are organised under the following headings:

A. Knowledge and Understanding
1. Standards for secondary specialist subjects.
2. Standards for primary subjects.
3. Additional Standards relating to early years (nursery and reception) for trainees on 3–8 and 3–11 courses.

B. Planning, Teaching and Class Management
1. Standards for primary English, mathematics and science.
2. Standards for primary and secondary specialist subjects.
3. Standards for secondary English, mathematics and science.
4. Standards for primary and secondary for all subjects:
   (a) planning
   (b) teaching and class management.
5. Additional Standards relating to early years (nursery and reception) for trainees on 3–8 and 3–11 courses.

C. Monitoring, Assessment, Recording, Reporting and Accountability

D. Other Professional Requirements

Each standard is set out discretely for clarity (see Appendix 1 of this book). However, the guidance from the TTA is that they can also be treated as a whole or grouped together. As the TTA says,

> Professionalism implies more than meeting a series of discrete standards. It is necessary to consider the standards as a whole to appreciate the creativity, commitment, energy and enthusiasm which teaching demands, and the intellectual and managerial skills required of the effective professional. (TTA 1999a, p. 12)

The standards are very demanding – they describe the best sort of teacher rather than a beginner. Colin Richards, in a letter to the *Times Educational Supplement*, wrote,

> The Standards represent an impossible set of demands which properly exemplified would need the omnicompetence of Leonardo da Vinci, the diplomatic expertise of Kofi Annan, the histrionic skills of Julie Walters, the grim determination of Alex Ferguson, and the saintliness of Mother Teresa, coupled with the omniscience of God. (*TES*, 7 January 2000)

One might think meeting standards that have already been met would be a straightforward matter. However, what a beginning teacher on a seven week teaching practice, with a stable class in a supportive setting with weekly observations and feedback can achieve, may be very different to what the same person could do in their first job. Many NQTs work in schools that are very different to the ones they experienced during their training. At one extreme someone's final teaching practice may have been spent in leafy suburbs or a village school, and then they find themselves working in a deprived inner city area.

Even in the most favourable conditions – where an NQT works in the school where they spent their teaching practice – things can be very hard. Everyone knows that some classes within a school are harder to teach than others. A new teacher finds it very hard to build an effective classroom environment out of a pile of furniture dumped in the middle of a bare room. In addition, there are the problems inherent in joining a new organisation, such as building relationships and understanding the politics of the staffroom. Some NQTs have difficult personal circumstances – many are starting their career with large loans to pay off and problems with accommodation are common.

The Induction Standards

As well as meeting the QTS Standards consistently, NQTs must meet the ten Induction Standards (see Figure 3.1). They are arranged under the same headings as the QTS Standards, but there are no further standards for knowledge and understanding.

A useful activity (see Activity 3.1) for induction tutors and NQTs is to analyse the Induction Standards in order to come up to a shared understanding of what they mean and what would constitute a satisfactory performance in each one.

In order to meet the Induction Standards, the NQT should demonstrate that he or she:

Planning, Teaching and Class Management
(a) sets clear targets for improvement of pupils' achievement, monitors pupils' progress towards those targets and uses appropriate teaching strategies in the light of this, including, where appropriate, in relation to literacy, numeracy and other school targets;

(b) plans effectively to ensure that pupils have the opportunity to meet their potential, notwithstanding differences of race and gender, and taking account of the needs of pupils who are:
● underachieving;
● very able;
● not yet fluent in English;
making use of relevant information and specialist help where available;

(c) secures a good standard of pupil behaviour in the classroom through establishing appropriate rules and high expectations of discipline which pupils respect, acting to pre-empt and deal with inappropriate behaviour in the context of the behaviour policy of the school;

(d) plans effectively, where applicable, to meet the needs of pupils with Special Educational Needs and, in collaboration with the SENCO, makes an appropriate contribution to the preparation, implementation, monitoring and review of Individual Education Plans;

(e) takes account of ethnic and cultural diversity to enrich the curriculum and raise achievement;

Monitoring, Assessment, Recording, Reporting and Accountability
(f) recognises the level that a pupil is achieving and makes accurate assessments, independently, against attainment targets, where applicable, and performance levels associated with other tests or qualifications relevant to the subject(s) or phase(s) taught;

(g) liaises effectively with pupils' parents/carers through informative oral and written reports on pupils' progress and achievements, discussing appropriate targets and encouraging them to support their children's learning, behaviour and progress;

Other Professional Requirements
(h) where applicable, deploys support staff and other adults effectively in the classroom, involving them, where appropriate, in the planning and management of pupils' learning;

(i) takes responsibility for implementing school policies and practices, including those dealing with bullying and racial harassment;

(j) takes responsibility for their own professional development, setting objectives for improvements, and taking action to keep up to date with research and developments in pedagogy and in the subject(s) they teach.

Figure 3.1 The Induction Standards (DfEE 1999 *The Induction Period for Newly Qualified Teachers* Circular 5/99)

Activity 3.1
Analysing the Induction Standards

Focusing on one standard at a time:

Discuss what you think it means. (This will involve unpacking its components.)

What would an NQT need to do to demonstrate that they were doing it:

  Well?

  Passably?

  Unsatisfactorily?

What help would an NQT need if they were not achieving the standard?

Make a list of any issues of debate.

© Sara Bubb 2000

Issues around the Induction Standards

There are some important issues concerning the Induction Standards which all involved should consider.

- Each standard is wide reaching.
- All the standards are open to interpretation, but some more than others.
- The success of an individual NQT depends largely upon the practice in their school.
- Many of the standards are cutting edge practice.
- NQTs must meet all the standards.
- The standards describe a perfect teacher.
- Some standards build on initial teacher training but others cover areas that will be new.
- There are no Induction Standards about subject and pedagogical knowledge and understanding.

Each standard is wide reaching
Although there are only ten additional standards for the induction year, each one is far reaching. For instance, induction standard (a), has many components that could be broken down like this:

- sets targets
- sets clear targets
- sets clear targets for improvement of pupils' achievement
- monitors pupils' progress
- monitors pupils' progress towards those targets
- uses appropriate teaching strategies

– uses appropriate teaching strategies in the light of this
– uses appropriate teaching strategies in the light of this in relation to literacy targets
– uses appropriate teaching strategies in the light of this in relation to numeracy targets
– uses appropriate teaching strategies in the light of this in relation to other school targets.

These components have to not only be in place but also must be demonstrated by the NQT.

All the standards are open to interpretation, but some more than others
The Induction Standards appear on the surface to be straightforward. It is only when one studies them in detail and tries to imagine what a good, average and unsatisfactory meeting of them would entail that their complexity becomes apparent. In my experience people interpret each standard differently. One that I think is particularly open to interpretation is standard (j):

> takes responsibility for their own professional development, setting objectives for improvements, and taking action to keep up to date with research and developments in pedagogy and in the subject(s) they teach.

This could mean anything from an occasional cursory reading of the front page of the *Times Educational Supplement* en route to the job pages, to doing research for a PhD.

Similarly, standard (f) requires NQTs to 'recognise the level that a pupil is achieving' but does not say which subjects and attainment targets this should be in. Some schools may interpret this as meaning levelling every child in every part of every subject of the curriculum. Others may settle for a focus on English and mathematics. Such disparity caused by lack of clarity is clearly unacceptable, yet this is the framework in which we have to work.

The success of an individual NQT depends largely upon the practice in their school
It has always been the case that individual teachers stand a greater chance of being effective in a well organised school, but for NQTs this becomes even more important. If the school has successful planning and target-setting procedures that all teachers are using, clearly the NQT will be at a huge advantage in meeting standards (a) and (b). The practice of other teachers and different levels of resourcing in schools are also an important factor, for example in meeting standard (e): 'The NQT should demonstrate that he or she takes account of ethnic and cultural diversity to enrich the curriculum and raise achievement.' NQTs who do not have good role models in other teachers and access to resources will be disadvantaged in trying to meet this standard.

Standards of pupils' behaviour vary enormously between schools and even classes. Some schools have more successful behaviour policies and procedures than others. Yet there would appear to be no allowances for this in the standards:

> (c) The NQT should demonstrate that he or she secures a good standard of pupil behaviour in the classroom through establishing appropriate rules and high expectations of discipline which pupils respect, acting to pre-empt and deal with inappropriate behaviour in the context of the behaviour policy of the school.

Similarly the number and range of pupils with special educational needs varies enormously between schools and classes. In some there are an enormous number of children with complex needs. This will obviously affect the meeting of standard (d):

> The NQT should demonstrate that he or she plans effectively, where applicable, to meet the needs of pupils with Special Educational Needs and, in collaboration with the SENCO, makes an appropriate contribution to the preparation, implementation, monitoring and review of Individual Education Plans.

An NQT's ability to meet this standard will depend also on the quality of the SENCO in the school, the use of outside agencies, and the time and help allocated to writing and reviewing IEPs.

Many of the standards are cutting edge practice

In many of the standards there is an emphasis on target setting, assessment and performance levels. These are deeply embedded in what is currently considered best practice. As such, they will be ahead of many teachers. This is good in that the new generation of teachers will be very effective. However, how can a new teacher be criticised for failing to do what his or her experienced colleagues are not doing?

What is a good enough meeting of the Induction Standards in a school where practice is far from up to date? Of course there is no bottom line clearly delineated.

NQTs must meet all the standards

There is no system of compensation, where excelling in one standard can compensate for weakness in another. There is no guidance about how to assess the Standards, how regularly they have to be met or what to do if they cannot be assessed because of the NQT's situation. Let us look at standard (b), for example:

> The NQT should demonstrate that he or she plans effectively to ensure that pupils have the opportunity to meet their potential, notwithstanding differences of race and gender, and taking account of the needs of pupils who are:
>
> • underachieving;
> • very able;
> • not yet fluent in English;
>
> making use of relevant information and specialist help where available.

We might wonder about the position of NQTs in a context such as a special school that does not allow them to demonstrate that they can plan for the very able. What if all the children an NQT teaches are fluent English speakers, of the same race and same gender? Should induction tutors arrange for them to visit schools where they can get these experiences? Again, there is no guidance.

The standards describe a perfect teacher

The standards are very demanding: they describe a perfect teacher rather than someone learning the trade. No one would argue with the need for the highest standards for the education profession, but it seems to me to be like expecting someone leaving medical school to be at brain surgeon level. In a way, that is what primary school teachers have to be – they are expected to teach a class like the teacher next door who has 20 years of experience. The children in both classes deserve the best education, but what can we realistically expect of someone at the start of their career?

There is no definition or description of what an NQT failing to meet a standard might look like. While there is probably agreement about what constitutes a very strong passing of the Standards, everyone will surely have their own ideas of what is good enough. There is no set of level descriptions for the Standards – though clearly they would be very useful – so that people could agree that an individual was on say level 3. However, until there are firmer guidelines some schools with very high standards might fail an NQT for not rigorously and consistently meeting every Induction Standard. A school with less high standards might pass the same NQT. Without guidance and moderation, the induction system could become enormously unfair. Inevitably, I suppose a common-sense professional judgement will have to suffice.

Some standards build on initial teacher training but others cover areas that will be new
Most of the Induction Standards build on those for qualified teacher status. The ease with which teachers meet the new standards will depend on things such as:

- How well the relevant QTS Standards were met during training.
- The calibre of their initial teacher training.
- The new context of a different school and class.
- The support they receive during the induction period.

Some standards, such as (g), (h) and (i), will however, be fairly new to the NQT. There will have been little opportunity for these on teaching practice. This has implications for the induction tutor who will have to ensure that support is given, for instance, in conducting parent interviews, writing reports, deploying support staff and additional adults in the classroom, and understanding and implementing school policies and practices.

There are no Induction Standards about subject and pedagogical knowledge and understanding
There are no further standards to do with subject and pedagogical knowledge and understanding, other than those covered by the QTS Standards. Indeed, there is no box on the induction assessment forms to say whether an NQT's subject knowledge is satisfactory. This seems absurd. Admittedly the QTS Standards do require a high standard of knowledge, but only in the core and specialist subjects. However, it seems bizarre that NQTs should not be expected to develop and refine their knowledge and understanding. They also need to develop their probably very basic knowledge of the other curriculum areas. As one of the NQTs on one of my courses wrote: 'You can never know enough'.

The 'good enough' newly qualified teacher

Winnacott (1971) wrote of the 'good enough' mother. As a teacher and later as a parent, I found this a very comforting idea. We all know what we should be – the perfect parent, partner, lover, child, sibling – but no one can be perfect all the time. Let us aim to be good enough – I'm sure we'll all feel happier! The QTS and Induction

---

Activity 3.2
The 'good enough' newly qualified teacher

In discussion with colleagues, make a list of the required characteristics of a 'good enough NQT'. Then think about what a 'not good enough teacher' would be like, so that you get a feel for the borderline area.

What differences are there between a good enough teacher and good enough newly qualified teacher?

How much match is there between your characteristics and the Standards for QTS and induction?

Were you and your colleagues in agreement about the characteristics of a good enough teacher? What are the implications of areas of dispute?

© Sara Bubb 2000

Standards make me shrivel with inadequacy because I'm not sure I'd meet them every day, even after 20 years in the job! Let us then consider what a 'good enough' teacher would be like (see Activity 3.2).

One group of induction tutors I worked with about six years ago decided that a good enough NQT would have many of the characteristics in Figure 3.2. They did not expect any one person to have all of them but felt that a 'not good enough' teacher would be noticeably lacking in a fair number. Interestingly, many of the characteristics are not mentioned in the QTS or Induction Standards. For instance, the induction tutors thought that liking children was of prime importance and yet this does not feature in the standards, possibly because it is hard to measure and maybe it is assumed to be a given. Yet, I have met teachers who do not particularly enjoy being with children of a certain age group. I think that it is useful to bear in mind what you consider a 'good enough' teacher to be when working with the Induction Standards.

The next chapter looks at the beginning of the induction process – the Career Entry Profile that NQTs bring to their first job. This gives crucial information about the NQT's route into teaching and their competency in terms of the QTS Standards.

Characteristics of a 'good enough' NQT

Likes and is interested in (rather than irritated by or scared of) the age group they teach.

Enthusiastic.

Flexible.

Open.

Can admit mistakes.

Wants to teach.

Works hard.

Respects the children, parents, support and teaching staff.

Reflective.

Can evaluate teaching and learning.

Listens well.

Approachable.

Has high but realistic expectations.

Stamina and good health.

Punctual.

Good attendance.

Well organised – especially in planning and preparation.

Knowledge of the curriculum.

Can manage children.

Sense of humour.

Works in a team but shows initiative.

Able to accept praise and positive criticism.

Confident.

Behaves professionally.

Performs legal duties.

Displays children's work.

Figure 3.2 Characteristics of a 'good enough' newly qualified teacher

4 The Career Entry Profile

The Profile

All students leaving training institutions in England after July 1997 have a Career Entry Profile (CEP). This is a black and white A4 booklet with an accompanying striped pink and purple booklet of Notes of Guidance and Standards. They are stored in an A4 sized pink and purple wallet. Both booklets need to be seen by the induction tutor, and NQTs are responsible for showing them to the school (see Chapter 1).

The CEP is completed at the end of a teacher training course, normally by the university tutor and student, and sent to the student's home address after it has been stamped and copied by the training institution. NQTs should have it in order to share it with the school as soon as they take up employment. Some NQTs that I have worked with reported a long delay in receiving the profile. This should be treated with some seriousness. It may not have been sent to the student because they have not actually been awarded qualified teacher status. Perhaps they have not passed all their written work. Some universities also insist that all debts are settled before granting the qualification. Whatever the issue, schools need to investigate absent CEPs.

The purpose of the Profile

The purpose of the Career Entry Profile is to help the transition from initial teacher training to a job in a school, by providing information in relation to the Standards for the Award of QTS about a new teacher's strengths and priorities for further professional development. It also requires new teachers to set objectives for professional development and develop an action plan for induction. As such, it is the primary tool of the induction tutor.

More specifically, the Career Entry Profile is intended to support induction tutors and NQTs, as they work together, to:

- make the best use of the skills and abilities the NQT brings with them;
- use the Standards for the Award of QTS and the Induction Standards to build on the new teacher's achievements;
- devise a focused and individualised programme of professional development, which will improve the NQT's practice in areas identified for development during the induction period;
- recognise the importance of effective professional development from the earliest possible stage in the NQT's career, and consider the new teacher's longer term professional development;

- make sustained and significant improvements in the quality of the new teacher's teaching in relation to the teacher's own objectives, the school's development plan, and local and national priorities. (TTA 1999a)

The NQT should make the Career Entry Profile available to the school and work with the induction tutor to use the profile in setting objectives for the induction period. The induction tutor is responsible for supporting the NQT and helping to implement a programme of monitoring, support and review based on the action plan set out in the Career Entry Profile.

The Career Entry Profile has three sections:

Section A. A summary of the NQT's initial teacher training, including any distinctive features of their training (completed by the ITT personal tutor and the NQT).

Section B. A summary of the NQT's strengths in four bullet points and four priorities for further professional development (agreed between the ITT provider and the NQT).

Section C. An action plan, including objectives, for the induction period (agreed between the school and the NQT).

Analysing the NQT's Initial Teacher Training

It is important to analyse the Career Entry Profile carefully and seek clarification from the NQT or training institution of any areas of confusion. The information about the training course on page 4 of the CEP is very important.

Training provider
This gives the name of the ITT provider or, for employment based routes, such as the Graduate/Registered Teacher Programme, the Recommending Body. Schools probably have views on the quality of local ITT providers, but more detail can be gained by reading inspection reports. The geographical area of the institution may also give important clues to the sort of schools and pupils the student came across on teaching practice. This will also alert you to NQTs who are new to the area, with all the problems that this entails.

Title of ITT programme
This gives the name of the course or programme leading to the award of QTS, e.g. BEd, PGCE, BA(QTS), Graduate Teacher Programme, Registered Teacher Programme.

Length of programme
This states the length of the programme, e.g. one year, 18 months, two, three or four years, or other. Remember, however, that the length of time spent in schools on teaching practice will be very similar. For instance, a PGCE student will have spent about 18 weeks in schools in a 39 week course, whereas a BEd student will have spent approximately 24 weeks in schools over a four year course.

Date of successful programme completion
This gives the month and year in which the award of QTS was recommended. The important consideration is whether this was before or after 7 May 1999. The statutory induction arrangements only apply to NQTs who qualified after this date. The TTA guidance is that those who qualified before this time would benefit from receiving similar programmes of monitoring, and support, but there is no obligation on schools or LEAs to provide this (TTA 1999b, p. 24). There is no limit on how much time there is between the award of QTS and the induction year, though obviously any gap will be an issue for consideration.

Be aware that students who did not train recently may not be up to date on recent initiatives. This may also be the case for BEd students because, for example, their mathematics component took place before the National Numeracy Strategy.

Age range
This shows the age range covered by the initial teacher training course. Hopefully this matches the age range of the school the NQT is working in.

Age range emphasis
This shows the age range emphasis in primary 3–11 and 5–11 courses. This will be the age range in which students did their teaching practices and specialised in. This is important since Circular 5/99 emphasises that NQTs should not be expected to teach outside the age range that they have been trained for (DfEE 1999, para. 26). If they are, they will need extra support.

Specialist subject(s)
All students will have specialised in one subject, in addition to the core subjects of English, mathematics, science, and information and communications technology. Often the specialism will be a foundation subject, but may be a core subject relating specifically to a particular phase such as Early Years. Further information about types of courses and their components can be found in Circular 4/98 (DfEE 1998a).

For primary, non-core, non-specialist subject(s)
These will typically be PE and RE, subjects in which the student has had some but not much training.

Other information about the initial teacher training programme
This might include distinctive features of school experience; additional qualifications gained during the course; special projects or extracurricular activities undertaken; and information about more limited coverage of National Curriculum foundation subjects. It is possible, for instance, that your NQT had little or no input in how to teach primary music, so you would want to address it in your programme of support.

Relevant experience gained outside initial teacher training would also be listed here. This could include any experience that has provided the NQT with skills and experience that will be of use in a teaching role, such as being a school governor, or previous employment in related fields.

Analysing the areas of strength and priorities for further professional development

The student and their tutor should agree four areas of strength in relation to the Standards for Qualified Teacher Status. These might refer to particular strengths in subject knowledge; planning, teaching and class management; assessment; and

Areas of strength	Priorities for further professional development
Good knowledge and understanding of mathematics, and ability to recognise and use connections across the subject in their teaching.	Develop subject and pedagogic knowledge in primary music beyond that covered during ITT course.
Ability to improve access to the curriculum for children with English as an Additional Language, by preparing high quality teaching resources and making effective use of commercial resources and support staff.	Develop confidence and skill in setting well-defined targets for improvement of pupils' achievement, and in monitoring and recording of progress towards these.
Confidence in the use of Information and Communications Technology in Art across the ability range, including with whole classes, small groups and individuals.	Ensure that homework and class work are integrated and that homework makes a direct contribution to learning objectives for all pupils.
Skilful use of questioning, in both plenary sessions and small groups, to elicit pupils' understanding and further their learning.	Improve management and structure of lessons to ensure that plenary activities are productive, that good use is made of summaries and that checks of learning are made against identified objectives.
Good feedback provided to pupils through discussion and marking, enabling pupils to understand what they have done well and how to improve further, and supporting the setting of clear targets.	Gain confidence and skill in communicating with parents and carers, and liaising with them to support pupils' learning.
Excellent use made of a wide range of assessment information in establishing challenging expectations for pupils' learning and for translating these into specific learning targets.	Maintain good discipline within consistent parameters/expectations without appearing too distant or unconcerned about individuals.
Good understanding of the needs of more able pupils, reflected in both planning and teaching.	Draw more effectively on assessment information in planning and teaching.

Figure 4.1 Examples of CEP strengths and areas for further development (TTA *Career Entry Profile*, p. 7)

professionalism. Judgements will usually have been made on the basis of the last teaching practice. The breadth of the areas of strength may give you insight into how well the student did in their last teaching practice.

Priorities for further professional development are areas in which the student has met the Standards for QTS but where further development would be beneficial. The examples in Figure 4.1, which have been taken from the CEP Notes of Guidance, have been included to illustrate the sorts of comments that might be written. They do not constitute one NQT's profile.

One significant feature of Career Entry Profiles that I have seen, is the variability of how the strengths and areas for development have been written. Some give a very clear picture. However, it is hard to understand what many of the statements actually mean because they are often written briefly and without a context. For instance, one NQT's areas for development were written in single word statements: Control, Music, Assessment, Parents. These are of little use to an induction tutor. Occasionally, areas are listed as both strengths and areas for development, which is very confusing. Some appear to have been written by the student without input from a tutor. All in all, the usefulness of this section in the CEP depends on the quality of writing of the person completing it. The strengths and areas for development need to be discussed with the NQT to find out exactly to what they refer. Understanding the context of the final teaching practice that the comments are based upon is all important.

Once in school, the induction tutor and NQT need to consider the statements made in Sections A and B of the profile, and look at them in the light of:

- the particular knowledge, understanding and skills needed to perform effectively in their new teaching post;
- meeting the Induction Standards;
- their aims for their longer-term professional development. Many NQTs are happy just to be teaching a class of their own, but others have a clear career plan. For instance, the NQT may want to become an English coordinator or educational psychologist and so would want to be gaining relevant experience.

It will be useful to the NQT to reflect on how confident they feel in teaching their first class by filling in a sheet such as Figure 4.2. This will help in setting objectives for the beginning of the induction period and planning an effective programme of monitoring, support and review.

Using the Career Entry Profile to set objectives for the induction period

Once you have analysed the NQT's strengths and areas for further development from their course, you need to think about the most useful objectives that will help them be a successful teacher in your school. Section C of the CEP, the Objectives and Action Plan, is at the core of the statutory induction arrangements. The objectives set for each NQT should be individual, and relate to the Induction Standards, the areas of strength and priorities for further professional development identified at the end of training, and the demands of their first post. The term 'objective' is used instead of 'target' to emphasise the world of professional development and to distinguish it from the target-setting practices in school relating to children's attainment.

Area	Reflection	Action
Arranging the classroom		
Year group		
Ability range		
Socio-economic profile of the children		
Pupils with SEN		
Pupils with little English		
Behaviour management		
Completing the register		
Deploying support staff		
Relating to parents		
Resources		
Teamwork		
School policies		
Assemblies		
Pupils with behaviour problems		
Child protection		
Planning using this school's formats		
Assessing using this school's formats		

© Sara Bubb 2000

Figure 4.2 How confident are you to teach your class? How do you feel your experiences so far have prepared you for teaching this class? Reflect honestly on the reasons for confidence or lack of confidence. You may feel unconfident because you have insufficient knowledge or resources, for instance. Try to think of some actions to be taken to address areas of weakness. This will help in setting up a programme of monitoring and support.

The first set of objectives should be agreed as soon as possible after the NQT is in post. These need to be decided in discussion with the NQT and be based ideally on an observation of teaching; evaluating plans, assessments and other documentation; and looking at the furniture, layout, etc. of the classroom. They will not automatically be the same as the CEP priorities for development. For instance, some CEPs highlight the need for input on music but if this is taught by a specialist in your school it would not need to be prioritised.

The way in which the objectives are framed will affect how achievable they are, and the ease with which progress towards them can be monitored and reviewed. They should be realistic and attainable. The NQT may be able to work towards most objectives on a day-to-day basis as part of their normal teaching role. Other objectives may involve the support of other school staff or expertise from outside the school.

Section C of the Career Entry Profile should record:

- the agreed objectives;
- the actions to be taken to achieve them, and by whom;
- the success criteria which will enable judgements to be made about the extent to which each objective has been met;
- the resources, if any, that will be needed;
- objective dates for their achievement;
- dates when progress will next be reviewed (likely to be the next formal review meeting). (TTA 1999a, p. 18)

Figure 4.3 is the TTA's example of how Section C, the objectives with action plan, can be completed. The black and white CEP has blank action plans on pages 7–10. I find it useful to enlarge these onto A3 paper. An alternative format for writing an action plan is shown in Figure 5.5. Figure 5.4 is an example of how this can be filled in.

In the next chapter I will look in more detail at setting objectives and the processes involved.

These examples are given to illustrate the kind of objectives that might be set for NQTs teaching a range of phases and/or subjects. They do not constitute one NQT's profile.

OBJECTIVE	ACTION TO BE TAKEN AND BY WHOM	SUCCESS CRITERIA	RESOURCES	TARGET DATE FOR ACHIEVEMENT	REVIEW DATE
To ensure effective use of classroom assistant in improving pupils' learning.	NQT to involve classroom assistant in lesson planning and include a section on the work of the classroom assistant in written plans. NQT to review impact of classroom assistant and discuss with classroom assistant and induction tutor.	Classroom assistant demonstrates clear understanding of role. Pupils working with classroom assistant achieve planned learning outcomes.	0.2 day for observation by induction tutor. 0.25 day for planning and review discussions between NQT, classroom assistant and induction tutor.	End of autumn term	12 December
To identify underachieving individuals and groups in classes taught, and develop strategies to provide targeted support.	Induction tutor to help NQT to use monitoring information to analyse performance of pupils in NQT's class, including by race and gender. Induction tutor to review reasons for underachievement and to observe NQT implementing strategies to address these.	NQT's planning and teaching reflects high expectations for all pupils. Underachieving individuals and groups make improved progress.	0.5 day for NQT to work on data analysis (including 0.2 release for support from induction tutor). 0.25 day for induction tutor to observe NQT's class and for post-observation discussion	End May	6 June
To provide clear information to parents that will enable them to be more fully involved in the support of children's learning.	NQT to discuss own preparation of next parents' evening with deputy head. NQT to review use of 'home—school contact books' with induction tutor and to develop strategies to improve their use.	Improved use of 'home—school contact books'. Effective communication at parents' evening.	0.2 release for deputy head to support preparation for discussion with parents. 0.2 release for induction tutor to review 'home—school contact books'.	End of spring term	4 April

Figure 4.3 Examples of objectives and action plans for the induction period (TTA *Career Entry Profile, p. 10*)

5 Setting objectives and drawing up an action plan

Issues around setting objectives

The benefit of setting objectives as a way to manage steady improvement by children and adults is well recognised. Objectives provide a framework for teachers doing a complex job at a very fast pace. They encourage people to prioritise tasks and make best use of time and other resources. NQTs should feel a sense of achievement when objectives are met.

There are problems, however, with setting objectives. One NQT said,

> 'What is the point of setting objectives? I have to be able to do *everything* to be able to teach at all. If my planning, control, assessment, teaching strategies or whatever are not right everything falls apart.'

She has a point. To be effective, all the QTS and Induction Standards have to be met.

Some NQTs find that there is discussion about how they are doing but no specific objectives. This is a missed opportunity. The very act of writing down objectives causes people to consider whether they are the real priorities and gives teachers something to focus on. Occasionally objectives are set without the complete agreement of the NQT. This is entirely counter-productive since the NQT is the one who has to be active in bringing about change so that they are met. Some have said that the orally-negotiated objectives change when written down.

Other NQTs have suffered from not having areas for development accurately diagnosed. It is very hard to decide what to work on when things are not going right because each problem has a huge knock-on effect. A frequent issue with objectives is that people are not specific enough, which inevitably leads to failure when they are not met. NQTs found that many objectives in the first term were too large and too long term so that they had to be repeated in the second term, but made more specific. Here is an example of one NQT's objectives:

First term:
To teach the National Literacy Strategy and National Numeracy Strategy effectively.

Second term:
To write focused learning objectives especially in the literacy hour and daily maths lesson.
To write specific group reading and writing objectives.
To plan more manageable independent work in the literacy hour and daily maths lesson.

Imagine how the NQT felt not to be able to meet the first term's objective! She would have made so much more progress had she been set the more detailed objectives in the first term. Always remember that objectives should be able to be met, while containing a degree of challenge.

Now look at Activity 5.1.

Activity 5.1

Think of your experiences with setting objectives. This may be related to pupils with SEN, appraisal or performance management.

What do you think of it as a way to develop?

How can you make it work for your NQT?

Tips for setting objectives

1. Think hard about the objective. Remember that your aim is to help the NQT meet the Induction Standards and to improve the quality of learning of their pupils. Each of us has our own idiosyncratic emphases, but these must not draw attention away from the Standards – whether we like them or not, they are the criteria upon which the NQT will be judged. So an induction tutor's love of beautiful displays or hatred of worksheets need to be subsumed into Standards on planning and teaching. The biggest factor to remember is whether the weakness is having a detrimental effect on children's progress.
2. Think always of the target setting dictum SMART. Objectives should be
   Specific
   Measurable
   Achievable
   Realistic
   Time-bound
3. The objective needs to be very specific. This is of course also true of learning objectives in lesson plans or objectives on an Individual Education Plan. Consider objectives such as:
   Improve subject knowledge in English
   Improve control
   Improve planning.
   These are too large, and will take a long time to achieve. It would be better to have a smaller, more specific aim.
4. Have no more than three objectives at a time. Some might be short-term, to be met within a week, and others would be longer-term objectives. Aim for them to be completed within a half term or perhaps less. This will encourage all involved to set realistic objectives and plan some useful actions that will enable them to be met.

5. It is encouraging if one of the three objectives can be to develop a strength. Imagine how depressing it would be a strength were to become a weakness! I have known, for instance, a student who had such good management skills with a very settled class on final teaching practice that these were considered a strength. Yet, the same person had huge problems with controlling a difficult class during the induction year.

6. It is important that NQTs feel ownership of the objectives. Ideally they should be jointly negotiated, with the NQT being proactive about identifying areas to develop, and how they can be achieved.

7. Remember to set objectives with successful NQTs. One can be tempted to leave them to their own devices, but they too deserve to be challenged.

The process of setting an objective and devising an action plan

When an NQT has a problem, it needs to be reflected upon and diagnosed accurately in order to draw up the most useful objectives and plan of action. I shall model how you could go about this with your NQT, using the very common problem of control.

1. The first thing to do when you have identified a problem is to brainstorm its features and results. For instance, Jenny's control problems include the following:

   - she lacks presence;
   - her voice is thin and becomes screechy when raised;
   - sometimes she comes down hard on the children and at other times she lets them get away with things;
   - she takes a long time to get attention;
   - she runs out of time so plenaries are missed, the class is late to assembly, etc.;
   - children call out;
   - children are too noisy;
   - a small group of children is behaving badly; and
   - even the usually well-behaved children are being naughty.

   Look at your list. Does it seem a fair picture? It is easy to be too hard or too generous.

2. List some positive features of the NQT, ideally relating to behaviour management. For instance, Jenny:

   - really likes and cares for the children;
   - speaks to them with respect;
   - plans interesting work for them;
   - is very effective when working with individuals or small groups;
   - has better control in the early part of the day; and
   - works hard.

3. With the NQT, think of when things go well and badly, as in Figure 5.1.

4. Discuss with the NQT why things go well using a format such as Figure 5.2. Reflection on successes is very powerful.

When things go well	When things go badly
At the start of the morning	Often after lunch time and playtimes. End of the morning.
At story-time	Tidying-up time
When I'm well prepared	Home time
When I've got a helper	When I'm on my own with the class
Literacy hour whole-class sessions	Literacy hour activities

Figure 5.1 Analysing when things go well and badly

When things go well	Why?
At the start of the morning	Children and NQT are fresh. Children and NQT know exactly what to do. NQT greets children well. Good atmosphere. Grudges are forgotten.
At story-time	NQT reads stories brilliantly, captivating children – they can't wait for the next episode.
When I'm well prepared	NQT feels confident when everything is well planned and resourced.
When I've got a helper	An extra person can focus on one table and keep an eye on another. NQT has a good relationship with the helper, shares planning with her and feels relaxed with her in the room.
Literacy hour whole-class sessions	NQT prepares these well, thinking carefully about use of big books, etc. Questioning and use of talk partners works well to involve all the children.

© Sara Bubb 2000

Figure 5.2 Analysing why things go well

When things go badly	Why?	Possible solutions
Often after lunch time and playtimes	Arguments outside the classroom spill into teaching time. NQT gets hassled trying to listen to everyone's point of view. This takes a long time, resulting in the rest of the class getting bored and restless. NQT loses teaching impetus.	Procedures for sorting out playground disputes?
Tidying-up time	Most children do nothing except mess around, leaving the tidying to the same few girls. Noise level rises.	New procedures for tidying?
Home time	Giving out reading folders, homework, letters, coats, etc., takes ages. Children get noisier. NQT gets stressed about being late out to the playground.	Planning systems for home time?
When I'm on my own with the class	The NQT is more inclined to panic when things go wrong when on her own. She starts shouting which increases the noise level and results in a sore throat.	Voice management? Planning?
Literacy hour activities	Hard to find useful activities that can be done independently. Some children finish too early but most barely start. Noise level rises. Children wander around distracting teacher from focus group.	Planning? Teaching independence?

Figure 5.3 Analysing why things go badly   © Sara Bubb 2000

5. The process of analysing strengths is very helpful and this positive thinking can now be used to reflect on problem parts of the day. Figure 5.3 shows a format that could be used to analyse in fine detail when things go badly. In your discussion, try to tease out the reasons for deterioration in control. Help the NQT think of actions to remedy situations – they can be surprisingly easy!

6. Try now to encourage the NQT to think more generally about behaviour management. What aspects are the most urgent and achievable? Select up to three objectives. Any more than three things to work on at a time becomes very difficult. An action plan (see Figure 5.4) needs to be drawn up to help the NQT meet the objective. Thinking about the steps towards an objective, and the action that they will involve will be essential. Some people have found the format (see Figure 5.5) useful for unpacking one objective, and prefer it to the CEP action plan (Figure 4.3).

Name: Jenny	Date: 1 November	Date objective to be met by: 13 December

Objective: To improve control, particularly after playtimes, in independent literacy activities, at tidying-up time and at home time.

Steps towards reaching the objective	Actions	When
To get attention more quickly	Brainstorm attention-getting devices Use triangle, etc., to get attention	ASAP
To avoid shouting	Voice management course Project the voice Don't talk over children	12 November Now
To plan for behaviour management, not just for learning	Glean ideas from other teachers through discussion and observation Write notes for behaviour management on plans	ASAP
To plan and implement new procedures for: sorting out disputes after playtimes, tidying, home time, independent literacy activities	Observe Y1 after lunch, in literacy activities, and at tidying-up and home times Glean ideas from other teachers Share new procedures with class and implement them	8 November ASAP

Support, monitoring and assessment of progress

Discuss progress and issues at induction tutor meetings.
Induction tutor to observe literacy hour on 29 November and feedback on 30 November.
SENCO to pop in after lunch and at home times at times during next fortnight to provide another pair of eyes on the problem. Will feedback at the time.

Progress notes:

Figure 5.4 An action plan to meet an objective – an example

Name:	Date:	Date objective to be met by:

Objective:

Steps towards reaching the objective	Actions	When

Support, monitoring and assessment of progress

Progress notes:

© Sara Bubb 2000

Figure 5.5 An action plan to meet an objective – blank

7. Progress towards the objective should be reviewed regularly and these reviews should result in the revision of objectives and updating of the action plan. In this way, monitoring and support will be well-focused throughout the induction period and ensure that short, medium and long-term needs are addressed.

Activity 5.2
Analysing some objectives

These are the objectives set for an NQT at the end of their first term. What do you like and dislike about them?

- Set clear aims at the beginning of every lesson and recap at the end to ensure that the children have made progress.

- Ensure that the lesson plan is referred to during the lesson and has clearly defined time limits to help inject pace and a sense of urgency into lesson.

- Ensure that on records of work and lesson plans there is evidence that assessment informs planning.

- To look at realistic methods of differentiation.

- To incorporate greater use of ICT into lessons.

- To carry out observations of staff in other curriculum areas.

© Sara Bubb 2000

We have looked at how objectives and action plans can be formulated to help NQTs solve behaviour management problems. In the next chapter I shall address problems that teachers have in planning.

6 Solving problems with planning

New teachers tend to have similar problems with planning. This is why it is useful for them to attend an induction programme, where they can focus on these problems and talk them through with others. Frequently experienced problems in planning include inadequate subject and pedagogical knowledge: what children need to be taught and how it should be taught to result in deep learning.

Subject knowledge

This is an area that all teachers find an issue. The number of changes, strategies and developments means that everyone is constantly having to deal with knowing new parts of the curriculum. Changing year groups and key stages increases the amount of subject knowledge needed.

NQTs have had a comparatively short amount of time to gain a great deal of knowledge. Some will come with greater knowledge of the most up-to-date thinking on some subjects than experienced colleagues. Others will have gaps in their knowledge because their course was not able to give certain subjects much attention. The QTS Standards are focused on English, mathematics, science and ICT which gives little time for anything else. The age range and subjects covered in teaching practices will also vary. Many NQTs will be teaching year groups that they did not teach on their final practice. Some may be teaching in a different key stage and so will need even greater help in getting to grips with the curriculum.

Pedagogy is also very important. Teachers need to know how children of different ages learn best, and to teach accordingly. One of the hardest things I did in my career was to take a reception class after teaching Year 6 for several years.

With all issues of subject knowledge it is essential to diagnose the problem accurately. This is best done by asking the NQT to evaluate their strengths and weaknesses using a format such as the one in Figure 6.1. This can be the focus of discussion. A programme of support and monitoring could include:

- self study – working through the National Literacy Strategy materials, for instance;
- planning partners, with the understanding that they will need to do a fair amount for the NQT at first;
- staff meetings;
- courses;
- discussion with subject coordinators; and
- observation of other teachers.

Area	Reflection on strengths and weaknesses	Action
Maths		
English		
Science		
ICT		
Art		
DT		
History		
Geography		
PE		
RE		
Music		

Figure 6.1 How do you feel your subject knowledge and experiences so far have prepared you for teaching this class?

Planning

Problems with planning have a very detrimental effect on all other areas of the Induction Standards. Here are some different types of problem that teachers may have with planning.

Types of problems with planning

1. Used to using different formats.
2. Needing to do more detailed planning than other teachers.
3. Doing too little planning.
4. Doing too much planning – and getting exhausted.
5. Imprecise learning objectives.
6. Activities not matching learning objectives.
7. Insufficiently high expectations.
8. Insufficient differentiation.
9. Not covering enough of the curriculum at sufficient depth.
10. Over-reliance on commercial schemes or other people's ideas.
11. Uses the activities suggested in team planning but does not think about how to do them.
12. Does not stick to year group plans.
13. Planning looks good on paper but the children make insufficient progress.
14. Weak parts of a generally satisfactory plan.

Now look at Activity 6.1.

Activity 6.1

Which of the problems above has your NQT had?

Have you met other teachers who have had any of these problems?

How did they overcome them?

Looking at the case studies below, what do you think of the objectives and actions set? What would you have done differently if the NQT had been yours?

© Sara Bubb 2000

Case studies

The following case studies illustrate different types of problems with planning – and possible remedies through objective-setting.

Case Study 1. Used to using different planning formats

Emma is confused by the different expectations and formats used on her teaching practice and in her present school. She is not comfortable with the school's formats and finds most boxes too small. She ends up using the school formats to keep the head teacher happy but uses her own more detailed ones as well. In effect she is duplicating work.

Objective
To use just the school's formats for planning by half term.

Action
Make the school's planning expectations and the reasoning behind them absolutely clear to Emma, using other teachers' work as examples. Ask her to talk through the differences between the school's and teaching practice planning formats. Does she have a point about the school's formats – are they as useful as they could be? Hopefully the discussion will enable Emma to see that the difference between the formats is fairly cosmetic.

Give feedback on the NQT's planning, showing how she can avoid duplication and where she can cut down the amount of writing. Make sure that she knows that it is perfectly all right to do extra planning where she feels it is necessary.

Case Study 2. Needing to do more detailed planning than other staff

Carol was used to doing more detailed written planning than experienced teachers in her school. The expectations for her planning as an NQT were not clear. Obviously she needed to plan to the same degree as other teachers in the school, but how much extra should she do? For instance, her school only required that the teachers plan their literacy hours on a weekly A3 sheet, whereas Carol had been used to writing a detailed lesson plan for each literacy hour. She felt that she should only use the A3 sheet and thought that there must be something wrong with her because she needed much more detail for the lesson to go well.

Objective
To reduce the time spent planning to X hours a week.

Action
Make sure that Carol understands the school's expectations for her planning, which are that she only needs to do what everyone else does, but that when she needs to write in more detail she should. Ask her to keep a record of how much time she spends on planning in a week, and try to reduce it gradually.

Boost her self-confidence by giving feedback on Carol's planning, preferably having seen a plan being taught. Identify where corners could be cut in writing her plans.

Case Study 3. Doing too little planning

Simon reacted against the stringent demands of college and his nagging tutor by doing too little planning, particularly because he did not have to show it to the head teacher. After an observation of a disastrous lesson his induction tutor asked to see the lesson plan. He pulled from his pocket an old envelope with some notes scribbled on it.

Objective
Plan teaching in accordance with school policy.

Action
Make planning expectations clear, using other teachers' work as examples.

Help Simon to see that lessons go better and children learn more when they are well planned.

Ensure that all planning is given to the head teacher at the beginning of every week, and returned if it lacks detail.

Case Study 4. Doing too much planning – and getting exhausted

Kate found it hard not to plan at teaching practice level. She soon filled lever-arch files with reams of paper and found that she was spending every waking hour planning and revising lessons. Although she handed weekly plans to the head teacher, she received no feedback on them. On teaching practice her plans were looked at in detail and commented upon regularly, and she found herself missing this.

Objective
To reduce the time spent planning to X hours a week.

Action
The head teacher to give feedback on planning. This will provide a much needed boost to Kate's confidence. Ask her to record how much time she spends on planning in a week, and try to reduce it gradually. Identify where corners could be cut in writing her plans.

Case Study 5. Imprecise learning objectives

Kevin wrote learning objectives on plans but they were insufficiently focused on what the children would be able to do by the end of the lesson. Here are a selection:
    Characteristic features of a period
    Instruction text – dissolving
    What is an atlas?
    To try to understand the idea of friendship
He did not break them down into smaller units. As a result, the children seemed to be doing activities rather than learning.

Objective
For all learning objectives to be so clear that they can be shared with children.

Action
Show Kevin how the learning objectives in other people's planning are phrased and arrange for him to observe a teacher who explains the lesson's objectives to the children. Monitor plans and give feedback emphasising the learning objectives.

Case Study 6. Activities not matching learning objectives

Beth did not think carefully enough about whether the activities she did with her Year 3 class were the best way of meeting her learning objectives. For instance, for the NLS objective 'to discuss characters' feelings, behaviour and relationships, referring to the text' she chose to use Mr Men books. (For those of you not familiar with these books, they are popular with preschool children and are about characters such as Mr Grumpy and Mr Noisy.) These have one dimensional characters – not quite what the authors of the NLS were intending!

Objective
To deepen understanding of literacy.
To plan activities that enable children to meet the learning objectives.

Action
Discuss planning with the English coordinator, and perhaps read some books containing ideas for Year 3 literacy. Beth should evaluate children's learning against the lesson objective to decide whether the activity enabled them to meet it.

Case Study 7. Insufficiently high expectations

Maureen worked in an inner city reception class with a high proportion of very needy children. She loved and cared for them well, but her planning showed low expectations. She planned few formal class or group sessions and had lots of free choice. In the taught group sessions objectives were often too easy. For instance, children were asked to count up to ten objects when they could have gone over 20. The class often misbehaved because they were insufficiently occupied.

Objective
To have high but realistic expectations of the class and plan accordingly.

Action
Arrange for Maureen to visit some other reception classes with children of similar backgrounds to see what can be achieved. She could also look at the work that the Year 1 class are doing to see where her children need to be in a year's time. If she spent some time finding out what her pupils can already do, she could plan activities that move their learning forward.

Case Study 8. Insufficient differentiation

Nick's planning met the needs of the majority of the class well but he did not cater for those who found learning difficult or those who were very able. Thus, in every lesson there were children off task because they were bored or worried, because the activity was either too easy or impossibly hard.

Objective
To differentiate activities so that the high attainers are challenged and the low attainers can make progress.

Action
Nick needs to assess the high and low attainers to discover what they can and cannot do, and then plan to meet their needs. His learning objectives could be differentiated by distinguishing between what all, some and a few children will achieve by the end of the lesson. He should differentiate the activities by outcome, task or the level of support. Looking at someone else's planning and teaching will help.

Case Study 9. Not covering enough of the curriculum at sufficient depth

Pam felt worried about gaps in her own knowledge of science. She had only a vague understanding of the concepts that were in the school's scheme of work for forces at Year 6. She did not have the time or resources to improve her understanding by reading. Instead, she resorted to giving the children commercial worksheets and often her science lessons were very brief.

Objective
To identify and address areas of weakness in subject knowledge of forces.
To plan work to cover the science curriculum in adequate depth for Year 6.

Action
Pam needs to identify what she does not understand about forces and then read some books to improve her knowledge. Children's books are often good at explaining concepts clearly. She should use books and ideas from the science coordinator to plan activities that aid children's learning.

Case Study 10. Over-reliance on commercial schemes or other people's ideas

Naseem felt very insecure. She planned with the other Year 4 teachers, who were very experienced and appeared much more knowledgeable than her. Overawed, she contributed little to the planning meetings and used all the others' ideas. Her lessons rarely seemed to go as well as her colleagues'. She was also over-reliant on activities and worksheets from commercial schemes rather than thinking of the needs of the individuals in her class.

Objective
To take a more active part at planning meetings, and plan some lessons for the rest of the team.

Action
Naseem needs to be more confident in planning. To help her, one would have to ascertain the reason for her lack of confidence. Is it because of weak subject knowledge?

She needs to be directed to some useful teachers' resource books to get ideas for planning and then think how activities could be used with her class. Her planning partners could encourage her ideas more and ask her to plan certain lessons. She should be encouraged to think not just about what the children are going to do, but why, how and when.

Case Study 11. Uses the activities suggested in team planning but does not think about how to do them

James followed the team planning in which he played an active part. He was confused when his lessons were deemed unsatisfactory by an OFSTED inspector who had given a very good grade to his colleague teaching the very same lesson. James was not used to thinking carefully about how to explain the learning objectives to the children and his input during the lesson was not as thorough or motivating as his colleague's. His class made less progress than the parallel classes during the term.

Objective
To plan in more depth, thinking about how to explain things to children to maximise their learning.

Action
James needs to see his colleagues in the parallel classes teach a lesson that he has taught to his class. He should reflect on the similarities and differences between his delivery and theirs, and put what he learns into practice.

Case Study 12. Does not stick to year group plans

Kit was a very extrovert, creative person who did not like being constrained by team planning. She would often change the activity that had been jointly decided, because she had thought of one that was more fun. The children loved their teacher, enjoyed every lesson and learned a great deal. One of them, however, had a twin sister in the parallel class. His parents complained that their children were having very different experiences at school, which they felt was an equal opportunities issue.

Objective
To understand the importance of joint planning and the need to share ideas that improve on the original planning.

Action
While one does not want to inhibit her creativity, Kit needs to realise that planning is done jointly to give children in the same year group similar experiences. She should be encouraged to share her good ideas with her colleague in the parallel class so that they can decide whether they should both change the activities.

Case Study 13. Planning looks good on paper but the children make insufficient progress

Prema kept a meticulous planning file and all her work was word processed. It looked very good, but her children did not make as much progress as in the previous year. During an observation, her induction tutor found that her teaching strategies and explanations were not being effective.

Objective
To assess what children learn and the progress they make.
To improve teaching strategies and explanations.

Action
Prema needs to understand that her children could be making better progress. She could observe another teacher using her plan with her class to see the different strategies and explanations they use.

Case Study 14. Weak parts of a generally satisfactory plan

Richard planned most of his lessons very well. It was only when his teaching was observed that the induction tutor realised that he was not planning plenaries. The children were not being reminded about the original learning objectives and were not asked to judge how well they had met them. Learning was not drawn together and lessons just fizzled out.

Objective
To plan and execute plenaries in all lessons.

Action
Richard should be praised for his good planning, but reminded of the value of plenaries. He could observe another teacher's plenary and look at how it was planned. His plenaries should always refer to the original learning objectives and children should be able to say how well they met them.

Planning for additional adults

Many classes have additional adults to support pupils with SEN, EAL, literacy and numeracy. Most are high quality, but some can prove to be a management issue. Here are some problems identified by NQTs (which you can think about in Activity 6.2):

- Being unsure of the additional adult's role.
- Not sure when they are going to be in the class.
- Not knowing what to ask them to do.
- Not wanting to ask them to do menial tasks.
- Some do too much for the children and encourage over-dependence.
- Some have poor grammar and spelling and so cannot help the children.
- Some have little control over the children.
- Some can take over the class.
- Some talk when the teacher has asked for everyone's attention.
- Some are stuck in their ways and do not like new ideas and practices.
- Finding time to talk to them to explain the activity.
- Planning for them, but they do not turn up.

Activity 6.2

Have you had any problems like this?

How did you remedy them?

What would you suggest an NQT do?

It is very hard for experienced teachers, let alone NQTs, to find time to talk to other adults who are working in the class. This often means that they are not used to best effect because the teacher needs to explain the activity and what they should do. A plan that can be given to them at an appropriate time should help this situation (see Figure 6.2).

NQTs should think about what they want the other adult to do during the whole-class teaching parts of the lesson. This could be a time to prepare resources or for them to be involved with certain children, checking their understanding for instance. Additional adults will want to know which children to support and where they should work. Most importantly, they need to know what the children should do, what they should do to help them and what the children should learn. Giving the adult a list of resources that they will need means that they can be responsible for getting them out.

Additional adults have important information about the children they work with. They often know more about the children with special needs, for instance, than the class teacher. These insights can be tapped by asking the adult to make some notes about how the children got on.

In the last two chapters we have considered some problems that many NQTs have and the sort of objectives and actions that could help them. In the next chapter I will describe the individualised induction programme of support, monitoring and assessment. This will help the NQT settle into your school, develop as a teacher and meet the standards at the end of the induction period.

Name: .... **Lesson:**.............................. **Time:** ....

What to do while I am whole class teaching

           Introduction: Plenary:

Children to support: **Where and when:**

Activity:

What the children should do:

What I would like you to do:

What I want them to get out of it:

Things that they will need:

How did they get on?

                                                        Thank you!

Figure 6.2 Plan for an additional adult in the classroom   © Sara Bubb 2000

7 The individualised induction programme

Planning the programme

The individualised induction programme is the key to successful progress for the NQT. Planning it is the main responsibility of the induction tutor. Because induction is now statutory, accountability is a very important issue. Although the numbers failing the induction year will be very small, all planning should be done with a worst case scenario in mind. Litigation may feature in such cases, since it will effectively mean an end to a teaching career. Documentation should have a high priority and be kept throughout the induction period.

Planning an effective programme is not easy. As we shall see, there are many components. There is no such thing as a perfect model because every context and every NQT are different. Even in the same school, what works for one NQT may not work for another. The statutory guidance emphasises that induction programmes should be 'tailored to individual needs'. My aim in this chapter is to give general principles and ideas for consideration as well as formats that can be adapted for individual contexts.

Support, monitoring and assessment

A significant feature of the statutory induction programmes is that they should involve 'a combination of support, monitoring and assessment'. In the past, support has been the focus of most programmes. Monitoring and assessment have been very much in the background. Clearly, support, monitoring and assessment are interrelated. In theory they could be separated, with a different person responsible for each area. However, this would not be the most effective way to encourage a teacher's development. This is not to say that one person has to provide all the support, monitoring and assessment. In the most successful schools all staff are involved in induction. The more people involved the better, as long as their input is planned and coordinated by one person. The induction tutor should coordinate input from other members of staff so that the NQT is not overloaded or gets contradictory advice, but concentrates on one thing at a time. See Activity 7.1.

There should be a balance between support, monitoring and assessment. Figure 7.1 illustrates the key stages throughout the induction period. I know of a school where the new teacher, Jane, was encouraged and nurtured by a warm and friendly mentor. Jane gained the impression that she was doing very well, but because there was no monitoring and assessment she did not actually make much progress. When told by

---

Activity 7.1
Support, monitoring and assessment

Think of the things that people would do when looking at a teacher's weekly lesson planning if they were in:

- a supporting role

- a monitoring role

- an assessment role.

Who in your school would be best placed to take these roles?

What are the issues for your school?

---

an inspector that her teaching was unsatisfactory, Jane was distraught and felt that she had been deceived by her school.

Another school took the task of monitoring and assessment very seriously. Tom was observed frequently by members of the senior management team and his planning and assessment were monitored weekly. This gave both Tom and the school a clear picture of how he was doing. However, he became overwhelmed by the pressure of assessment. There was little support to help him address his weaknesses in behaviour management, which he felt were enormous. Nobody helped him set in place the many little things that would make a difference. Tom progressively lost confidence, his control deteriorated, and eventually he resigned after a period of sick leave.

Before the NQT starts teaching

Preliminary documentation
The induction process starts as soon as an NQT is appointed. As well as their job description, contract, arrangements for salary payments, pension contributions and procedures for sick leave, they should be sent documentation to get a feel for the school. This would include the following, though items might be prioritised or staggered to avoid overload.

- School prospectus.
- Staff handbook or something that details things such as how to complete the register, school and playground rules, planning formats.
- Teaching staff list – professional and staffroom names, classes taught and responsibilities.
- Support staff list – professional and staffroom names and responsibilities.
- Administrative staff list – professional and staffroom names and responsibilities.
- Curriculum policies.

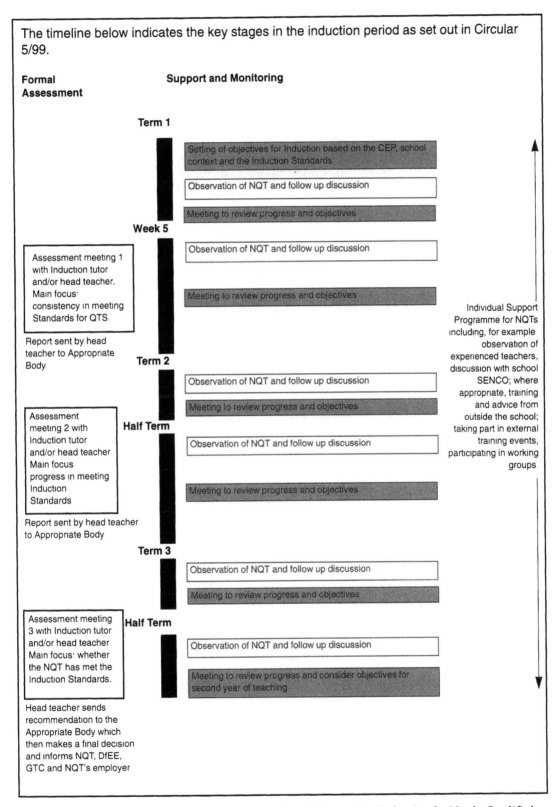

The timeline below indicates the key stages in the induction period as set out in Circular 5/99.

Formal Assessment

Support and Monitoring

Term 1

Setting of objectives for Induction based on the CEP, school context and the Induction Standards

Observation of NQT and follow up discussion

Meeting to review progress and objectives

Week 5

Observation of NQT and follow up discussion

Meeting to review progress and objectives

Assessment meeting 1 with Induction tutor and/or head teacher. Main focus: consistency in meeting Standards for QTS.

Report sent by head teacher to Appropriate Body

Term 2

Observation of NQT and follow up discussion

Meeting to review progress and objectives

Half Term

Assessment meeting 2 with Induction tutor and/or head teacher. Main focus: progress in meeting Induction Standards

Observation of NQT and follow up discussion

Meeting to review progress and objectives

Report sent by head teacher to Appropriate Body

Term 3

Observation of NQT and follow up discussion

Meeting to review progress and objectives

Assessment meeting 3 with Induction tutor and/or head teacher. Main focus: whether the NQT has met the Induction Standards.

Half Term

Observation of NQT and follow up discussion

Meeting to review progress and consider objectives for second year of teaching

Head teacher sends recommendation to the Appropriate Body which then makes a final decision and informs NQT, DfEE, GTC and NQT's employer

Individual Support Programme for NQTs including, for example observation of experienced teachers, discussion with school SENCO; where appropriate, training and advice from outside the school; taking part in external training events, participating in working groups.

Figure 7.1 Overview of the Induction Process (TTA *Supporting Induction for Newly Qualified Teachers. Part 1: Overview*)

– Curriculum schemes of work relevant to the NQT's year group.
– Other policies (health and safety, bullying, child abuse, etc.).
– Timetable – assemblies, playtimes, lunch times, hall and playground spaces, meetings.
– Diary sheet of school events.

The initial visit

The head teacher should arrange, where possible, for NQTs to visit the school to familiarise themselves with the environment and meet the class or classes which they will be teaching. This visit is important in making the NQT welcome, and introducing them to colleagues and school procedures. NQTs should leave the school feeling full of enthusiasm, with lots of information and secure in the knowledge that they will be supported.

I have, however, known people to return from these visits so worried that they speak of not signing contracts. Impressions of the school gained at interview have been contradicted by talking to jaded teachers, and seeing the reality of difficult children and poor organisation. Every year, there are one or two NQTs who do not turn up at their school or who leave after the first week. This can be avoided by preparing for the initial visit carefully, though this is often the last thing anyone feels like doing at the end of a demanding term. Part of this preparation will involve sharing the aims of the visit with all staff and encouraging them to be positive and friendly. Everyone should know what the NQT has already been sent so that they can expect relevant questions. Now look at Activity 7.2.

Activity 7.2

Think about your initial visit to your first school.

What was helpful?

Did anything put you off?

What lessons can be learnt from your experience?

© Sara Bubb 2000

The following is a checklist for drawing up a timetable for the NQT's initial visit. The NQT should:

- Meet the children they will be teaching.
- Get a feel for the standard of work of the children (high, average, and low attainers) that they will be teaching.
- Look at class records.
- See their classroom.

- Look at resources in their classroom.
- Look at resources in the school.
- Look at the local environment.
- Become familiar with routines and procedures.
- Meet all teaching, administrative and support staff.
- Spend some time with key people:

  - Head and deputy
  - their class's present teacher
  - induction tutor
  - teachers who they will be planning with
  - year and/or phase group coordinator
  - SENCO
  - support staff with whom they will be working
  - premises officer
  - secretary.

At some time before or during the first week, the induction tutor needs to agree a programme with the NQT based on the Career Entry Profile. Further advice on how to use this document is provided in Chapter 4.

Advantages of joining an external induction programme	Disadvantages of joining an external induction programme
The NQT will meet many others from different schools and training institutions.	NQTs may become dissatisfied with their school when they hear about others.
They should meet general needs well, easing the burden on schools.	The school can meet individual needs in their specific context.
Economy of scale should mean value for money.	With a limited budget the money might be better spent.
NQTs will learn from the practice of other schools and teachers.	It may not be feasible for several NQTs from the same school to be out at the same time.
There will be time to reflect out of the school.	The time taken travelling to the courses may not be practical.
The programme will cover subjects and topics that the school may not have the time or expertise to deliver.	The school may have staff with the time to run sessions that are focused on the NQT's individual context.
Many have tasks to do after sessions that encourage reflection and develop practice.	
Some courses are accredited so that NQTs can move towards getting an Advanced Diploma or MA.	

Figure 7.2 Advantages and disadvantages of joining an external induction programme

Joining an externally organised induction programme

One important decision that needs to be made early on is whether the NQT should join a programme with others. Figure 7.2 summarises the advantages and disadvantages of joining an externally organised induction course. These are often run by local education authorities, higher education institutions and educational consultants. The big advantage of joining such a programme is that NQTs gain a great deal from talking to each other. They feel enormously comforted by hearing that others are going through the same problems. No matter how sympathetic experienced members of staff are, the solitary NQT in a school often feels that they are the only ones who cannot, for instance, get their class to assembly on time. Enrolment on an externally organised programme also eases the burden on schools to provide training. However, it can only supplement the individualised school programme – not replace it.

The choice of which programme to join is also a matter for consideration. Many will also run training for induction tutors. As soon as schools know they will be employing an NQT, they can start researching the options. Quality and value for money are all important. There are the obvious benefits from attending the local programme: the

Date, time and venue	Subject	Things learnt that will influence classroom practice

Figure 7.3 Record of training (in and out of school) attended by the NQT © Sara Bubb 2000

NQT will become familiar with local advisers and initiatives and meet teachers from similar schools. Programmes run by HEIs or other LEAs may, however, be at a more convenient time and location or prove to be better value for money.

Many induction courses have tasks for the NQT that encourage reflection on their development after specific sessions. The school programme should also expect some evidence of reflection on externally organised courses. Figure 7.3 provides a format for this. School-based INSET can be reflected upon in a similar way.

Components of the induction programme

The induction programme should have specific weekly events, involving support, monitoring and assessment. The filling in of a diary sheet such as the one in Figure 7.4 will help the induction tutor and NQT plan and briefly record specifics. It can be used for evaluating the programme, and as a record to show the Appropriate Body and other external monitors.

The school-based programme has several elements that need to be seen as a whole in contributing to the NQT's development:

- observation of the NQT teaching;
- school staff meetings and INSET;
- the focus of the 10 per cent release time; and
- meetings with the induction tutor.

I shall look at each of these components in turn.

Observation of the NQT teaching

This is clearly a key element in the induction process. The TTA (1999b) recommends that NQTs should be observed formally every half term. These and other observations should be arranged well in advance. Further guidance can be found in Chapter 8.

School staff meetings and INSET

School staff meetings and INSET will also have an impact on the NQT's progress and so should be recorded weekly. As with any teacher, NQTs should be encouraged to reflect on what they have learned and how this has affected their practice. This can be done briefly through using the format shown in Figure 7.5.

How to spend induction release time

> The 10 per cent remission from teaching duties should be used for the NQT's induction programme. It should not be used as unspecified non-contact time nor should it be used to cover the teaching of absent colleagues. The release time should be over and above any time normally assigned to teachers in a school for activities such as planning and marking and should be used for a targeted and coherent programme of professional development, monitoring and assessment activities. TTA (1999, p. 128)

Of particular importance is the planning of the 10 per cent release time designated for induction. This should be used specifically for the NQT's professional development.

NQT:

Induction tutor:

Objectives:

Week beginning... Observation of NQT	NQT release time for induction	Induction tutor meetings	Staff meetings and INSET

Figure 7.4 The Induction Programme Diary

© Sara Bubb 2000

Date/ time	Activity	Purpose	Reflection

© Sara Bubb 2000

Figure 7.5 Reflection on induction time activities

A record should be kept of how the time is spent. The NQT should be encouraged to reflect upon their induction experiences. This can be done in a number of ways. All activities should have a clear purpose. This will be the focus of the reflection, but inevitably there will be other unplanned gains. Reflection is most valuable when it occurs in dialogue, so it would be useful to spend some of the induction tutor meetings discussing what the NQT learnt from their release time. Other means of reflection could be using a format such as the one in Figure 7.5.

Ways to spend release time
There are many different ways to spend induction time, some of which are listed below.

1. Reflecting on progress so far.
2. Attending induction and other courses.
3. Observing other teachers in the school.
4. Observing teachers in other schools.
5. Observing someone teach the NQT's class.
6. Observing how children of different ages learn.
7. Looking at resources in the school, such as computer programmes.
8. Visiting local education centres, museums and venues for outings.

9. Looking at the educational possibilities of the local environment.
10. Working with the SENCO on writing and reviewing individual education plans.
11. Reading pupils' previous records.
12. Making some in-depth assessments of individual children.
13. Improving their subject knowledge through reading, observation, discussion, etc.
14. Analysing planning systems in order to improve their own.
15. Analysing record keeping systems in order to improve their own.
16. Planning a lesson based on the thorough assessment of pieces of work.
17. Making resources.
18. Learning more about strategies for teaching the children with special educational needs in their class.
19. Learning more about strategies for teaching the children with English as an additional language in their class.
20. Learning more about strategies for teaching the very able children in their class.

Meetings with the induction tutor

It is essential that the NQT has meetings with their induction tutor, to plan their programme and be supported.

When should meetings take place?
There should be regular planned meetings with the induction tutor. These should happen throughout the year. It is very easy to let them slide because of other demands on time, but NQTs really do benefit from attention, particularly because of the formal assessment at the end of each term. Often successful teachers are left to their own devices – but they too need to be challenged in order to become even better teachers.

Induction meetings should have high status in the school. Ideally they should happen during the school day. If the induction tutor is not class based, this could happen during the NQT's release time. It is, unfortunately, more usual for meetings to be held after school. This in itself is often a problem in many schools because of the number of other meetings and courses that both parties need to attend. However, it is important that they do take place, perhaps taking priority over other meetings.

How often should induction meetings take place?
The answer to this question will depend on how much support the NQT is getting from others. For instance, year group planning and assessment meetings will be of enormous benefit to an NQT. Similarly, if they make friends with someone on the staff with whom they can discuss issues, this will ease the burden on the induction tutor – as long as advice from different quarters is not contradictory. NQTs will also vary in the amount of support they and you think they need. Generally, I would recommend weekly meetings at first, maybe reducing to fortnightly after the first term. The TTA framework (1999b, p. 6), however, implies a minimum of a meeting at the beginning and end of each half term.

How long should meetings last?
Meetings should consist of quality time. Chats in the staffroom at playtime may be pleasant but cannot take the place of planned meetings. These help to protect both parties. Some NQTs are extremely demanding, wanting to talk about their

experiences every day. A regular meeting slot of up to an hour will be seen as the appropriate time to raise matters. Quality time induction meetings should have:

- no interruptions – the venue needs to be chosen to minimise disturbances from phone calls, children, other teachers, etc.;
- a fixed start and finish time, with about an hour in between;
- an agreed agenda, albeit informal and flexible;
- an agreed aim, probably linked to the Induction Standards;
- a focus on the NQT, rather than the induction tutor's anecdotes;
- a record of any agreed outcomes.

What should be the focus of induction meetings?

The NQT's progress in relation to the Standards should be the main focus of meetings. The TTA (1999b, p. 6) suggests that the first term's assessment focus should be the meeting of Standards for QTS in the context of the new school and class. Assessment in the second and third terms should focus on progress against the Induction Standards. It is useful if both the induction tutor and NQT have a record of their meetings. Figure 7.6 has proved a useful format for many induction tutors attending my courses.

Induction meetings should have an opportunity for feedback on recent induction events and there should be ongoing discussion about progress against the objectives. Other areas to look at might include those listed in Figure 7.7. When looking at the list, consider which activities could be delegated and to whom. What areas should be the definite domain of the induction tutor?

This list is enormous, but the NQT will be confident in many areas following their initial teacher training. Some activities can be delegated to other members of staff. The NQT can address areas during their release time. Some subjects will be covered in staff meetings and external induction programmes.

Lastly, Figure 7.8 (pp. 68–73) is an example of one NQT's induction programme with their half-termly objectives. It shows how all the elements can be brought together in a manageable way, and how the programme can respond to the NQT's stages of development through the year. Do Activity 7.3 to focus your thoughts while looking at Figure 7.8.

Activity 7.3
Analysing an individual induction programme

What do you think of the programme?

How does it develop over the year?

Do the activities and meetings correspond to the objectives?

How do staff meetings contribute to the NQT's development?

How many times is the NQT observed and by whom?

Which standards are covered in the programme?

How does Trina's programe compare to your NQT's?

Record of Induction Meeting
Participants: Date and time:
Agenda
Things that are going well
Things to improve
Progress on current objectives
Objectives and action plans Short-term   Longer-term
Date of next meeting:
Focus of next meeting
Signatures

Figure 7.6 A record of induction meetings

Classroom organisation	Stress management
Behaviour management	Events – harvest, festivals
Managing transitions	Class assemblies
Planning	Organising class trips
Assessment	PE – using the school's apparatus
Levelling children's work	Child protection
Record keeping	Teachers and the law
Working with additional adults	SMSC
Dealing with parents	Report writing
Parents' evenings	Pupils with EBD
SEN	Circle time
Very able pupils	Bullying
EAL	Health and Safety
Voice management	Teaching strategies

Every area of the Curriculum:

English	ICT	PE	Geography
Mathematics	RE	Art	Music
Science	DT	History	

Figure 7.7 Areas to focus on during induction tutor meetings and release time

Trina's Induction Programme – 1st half of Autumn term

Objectives: To organise the classroom to ensure effective learning.
To improve behaviour management.

Week beginning observation of NQT	NQT release time for induction	Induction tutor meetings	Staff meetings and INSET
6 September	10 Sept. LEA induction programme – The Standards. Relating to parents.	The Career Entry Profile.	2 days Numeracy training.
13 September	Observe Y2, focusing on organisation.	Classroom organisation.	General.
20 September Observation focusing on organisation and control.	Observe Y1, focusing on organisation and behaviour management.	Feedback and discussion following observation.	Numeracy planning.
27 September	29 Sept. LEA induction programme: Classroom management.	Behaviour management.	General – harvest festival arrangements.
4 October	Prepare for parents' evening. Display.	Monitor planning.	Numeracy assessment.
11 October Observation by maths coordinator.	Observe own class being taught by supply teacher.	Feedback following observation by maths coordination.	Review behaviour policy.
18 October	Observe PE specialist take own class for gymnastics.	Review of the half term objectives. Set new objectives.	Review behaviour policy.

Figure 7.8 An example of an Individualised Induction Programme for a Year 2 teacher

Trina's Induction Programme – 2nd half of Autumn term

Objectives: To increase pace in lesson introductions.
To plan for pupils of different attainment, especially those with SEN.

Week beginning observation of NQT	NQT release time for induction	Induction tutor meetings	Staff meetings and iNSET
1 November	Observe Y5, focusing on pace in maths.	Plan programme of how to spend induction time.	Numeracy.
8 November	LEA induction course: Behaviour management.	SEN with SENCO.	SEN policy review.
15 November Observation focusing on pace in introductions and differentiation.	Observe Y3, focusing on pace and differentiation in literacy hour.	Feedback following observation. Monitor children's work.	General.
22 November	Look at SEN resources and extension activities.	Review SEN IEPs with SENCO.	Numeracy.
29 November Observation by head teacher.	LEA induction course: Planning for pupils with SEN and high attainers.	Feedback following observation by head teacher.	Arrangements for Christmas.
6 December Assessment meeting with head teacher and induction tutor.	Reflection time – fill in the self-evaluation sheet of strengths and areas for development.	Assessment meeting with head teacher and induction tutor.	End of term assessments.
13 December	End of term assessments.	Review of the half term objectives. Set new objectives.	

Figure 7.8 continued

© Sara Bubb 2000

Trina's Induction Programme – 1st half of Spring term

Objectives: To improve procedures for assessment to inform planning.
To develop target-setting in English and mathematics.

Week beginning observation of NQT	NQT release time for induction	Induction tutor meetings	Staff meetings and INSET
3 January	Detailed assessments of 4 children in the class.	Plan the induction programme.	General.
10 January	LEA induction course: Assessment 1.	Assessment coordinator.	Numeracy.
17 January	Write group targets for writing and reading.	Assessment coordinator monitors assessment file.	Planning book week.
24 January Observation focusing on target-setting and assessment.	Observe nursery – focus on target-setting procedures.	Feedback from observation.	Target-setting.
31 January	LEA induction course: Managing pupils with emotional and behavioural difficulties.	Discuss video clips of whole-class teaching to help pace.	Children's literature.
7 February	Set group targets for maths.	Maths coordinator – targets.	General.
14 February	Observe Y6, focusing on target-setting.	Review of the half term objectives. Set new objectives.	Numeracy.

Figure 7.8 continued   © Sara Bubb 2000

Trina's Induction Programme – 2nd half of Spring term

Objectives: To deploy additional adults to make best use of their time for children's learning.
To explore and use multicultural resources.
To evaluate progress of different groups within the class.

Week beginning observation of NQT	NQT release time for induction	Induction tutor meetings	Staff meetings and INSET
28 February	Observe Y2 in Beacon school, focusing on use of additional adults and multicultural resources.	Plan the induction programme.	Review Child Protection and Health and Safety policies.
6 March	Observe YR, focusing on the deployment of other adults.	Assess the NQT's planning folder.	General.
13 March	LEA induction courses: PE; Record keeping.	Discuss progress of children through looking at their work.	Science.
20 March	LEA training course for Y2 tests.	Discuss multiculturalism.	Science.
27 March Observation by English coordinator.	Observe YR in Beacon school, focusing on use of additional adults and multicultural resources.	Feedback from observation.	Discuss bullying policy.
3 April Assessment meeting.	LEA induction course: Assessment 2.	Assessment meeting.	Science.
10 April	Write SEN IEPs.	Review of the half term objectives. Set new objectives.	Design and Technology workshop.

© Sara Bubb 2000

Figure 7.8 continued

71

Trina's Induction Programme – 1st half of Summer term

Objectives: To carry out Key Stage 1 tests on the class.
To decide what level each child is working at in English, mathematics and science.

Week beginning observation of NQT	NQT release time for induction	Induction tutor meetings	Staff meetings and INSET
1 May	Observe Y6, focusing on end of KS2 levels.	Plan the induction programme.	Agreement trialling.
8 May	Level children's work in English, Maths and Science.	SATs preparation	Agreement trialling.
15 May Observation by induction tutor.	Observe Y6 doing NC tests.	Feedback from observation.	Discuss SATs tests.
22 May	LEA induction course: Reporting to parents.	Review of the half term objectives. Set new objectives.	General.

Figure 7.8 continued   © Sara Bubb 2000

Trina's Induction Programme – 2nd half of Summer term

Objectives: To write clear and informative reports for parents.
To conduct parents' evening confidently.
To plan outing.

Week beginning observation of NQT	NQT release time for induction	Induction tutor meetings	Staff meetings and INSET
5 June	Observe Y4.	Plan the induction programme.	Report writing formats.
12 June Observation by induction tutor.	Observe Y1 and Y2 in Beacon school, focusing on good practice.	Feedback from observation. Reading reports.	Mathematics.
19 June	LEA induction course: Professional development – being a curriculum coordinator.		Mathematics.
26 June Observation by head teacher.	Preliminary visit to farm to prepare for class trip.	Feedback from observation.	General.
3 July	Prepare for class trip, using school policies.	Planning an outing.	Review literacy hours.
10 July Final assessment meeting.	Gathering evidence for the final assessment meetings.	Final assessment meeting. Set objectives for second year.	Planning for next year.
17 July	Looking at new class and their records.		

© Sara Bubb 2000

Figure 7.8 continued

Monitoring an NQT's progress is an essential part of any induction programme. The next chapter describes ways to record evidence by looking at how to analyse planning, assessment, samples of children's work and, very importantly, how to make observations of their teaching.

8 Ways to record evidence of progress

Induction tutors need to monitor the NQT's progress towards meeting the Standards and use this information to inform the termly assessment forms. There are different ways to do this. Observation of teaching is a crucial form of evidence, but cannot be used to monitor all the Standards. Figure 8.1 highlights some of the different forms of evidence for each standard.

Clearly, in most primary schools induction tutors can gain a good idea about the quality of a teacher through their everyday behaviour and work. Most of the staff will be involved with the NQT to some degree and their views should be taken into account. Planning partners, the SENCO and special needs assistants working with the NQT's pupils will have particularly important perspectives, for instance. However, one must avoid basing judgements on anecdotal evidence and hearsay – particularly if these are negative.

Analysing a teacher's planning and assessments

Analysing a teacher's planning and assessments can be very difficult, especially if they teach a year group that you are not experienced in. It is best done by the year or phase group coordinator, if the school has one. I have designed some formats (see Figure 8.2 for monitoring planning and Figure 8.3 for monitoring assessment) with general prompts that could be used to structure the monitoring. These could be adapted for the individual NQT's context. They may best be done with the NQT so that they can direct you to where evidence lies.

Summative and ongoing formative assessments will probably be kept in different places, depending on the age of the children and the school's and teacher's systems. Here are some places where evidence for Monitoring, Assessment, Recording, Reporting and Accountability might be:

- Assessment folder
- Baseline assessments
- Records of achievement
- Marking in children's exercise books
- Targets in children's exercise books
- Teacher's mark book
- Lesson evaluations
- Group reading records
- Guided writing records
- Reading folder
- Home–school reading diary
- IEPs
- Behaviour book
- Significant achievement book
- Letters to parents
- Reports

Rather than looking at the whole class, you might find it more useful to look at the assessments of just a few children. Choose a high, average and low attainer and a child with English as an additional language, for instance.

Induction Standards (TTA Career Entry Profile)	Forms of evidence
(a) Sets clear targets for improvement of pupils' achievement, monitors pupils' progress towards those targets and uses appropriate teaching strategies in the light of this, including, where appropriate, in relation to literacy, numeracy and other school targets.	Planning. Assessment file. Observation. Pupils' work.
(b) Plans effectively to ensure that pupils have the opportunity to meet their potential, notwithstanding differences of race and gender, and taking account of the needs of pupils who are: • underachieving • very able; • not yet fluent in English; making use of relevant information and speicalist help where available.	Planning. Observation. Pupils' work.
(c) Secures a good standard of pupil behaviour in the classroom through establishing appropriate rules and high expectations of discipline which pupils respect, acting to pre-empt and deal with inappropriate behaviour in the context of the behaviour policy of the school.	Observation. Display of class rules.
(d) Plans effectively, where applicable, to meet the needs of pupils with Special Educational Needs and, in collaboration with the SENCO, makes an appropriate contribution to the preparation, implementation, monitoring and review of Individual Education Plans.	Planning. Assessment file. Observation. IEPs. Pupils' work. Discussion with SENCO.
(e) Takes account of ethnic and cultural diversity to enrich the curriculum and raise achievement.	Planning. Looking at the classroom.
(f) Recognises the level that a pupil is achieving and makes accurate assessments, independently, against attainment targets where applicable, and performance levels associated with other tests of qualifications relevant to the subject(s) or phase(s) taught.	Assessment file.
(g) Liaises effectively with pupils' parents/carers through informative oral and written reports on pupils' progress and achievements, discussing appropriate targets and encouraging them to support their children's learning, behaviour and progress.	Reports. Letters to parents. Notes from parents evenings.
(h) Where applicable, deploys support staff and other adults effectively in the classroom, involving them, where appropriate, in the planning and management of pupils' learning.	Planning. Observation.
(i) Takes responsibility for implementing school policies and practices, including those dealing with bullying and racial harassment.	Observation in lessons and around the school and playground.
(j) Takes responsibility for their own professional development, setting objectives for improvements, and taking action to keep up to date with research and developments in pedagogy and in the subjects they teach.	Discussion. Self-reflection. Behaviour in meetings.

© Sara Bubb 2000

Figure 8.1 Ways to monitor the NQT's progress

Prompts for monitoring planning	Comments
Is the planning organised suitably in a file?	
Do plans cover the whole curriculum?	
Is the teacher following the school planning policies and practices?	
Can you track work through long, medium and short-term plans?	
Are useful links made between subjects, to aid children's learning?	
Is the planning covering the same work as parallel classes?	
Does the planning show appropriate expectations?	
Is the right amount of work being planned for the time allocation?	
Has the NQT drawn up a suitable timetable for when different work is to be done?	
Are learning objectives clear?	
Are there different learning objectives and/or activities to allow children of different attainment to make progress?	
Does the planning take into account the needs of pupils who are not yet fluent in English?	
Do the activities enable objectives to be met?	
Are the resources and activities appropriate and interesting?	
Are there planned assessment opportunities?	
Are plans informed by assessing children's knowledge, skills and understanding?	
Are lessons evaluated?	

Figure 8.2 Monitoring a teacher's planning

Prompts for monitoring assessment	Comments
Are assessments organised suitably?	
Are record keeping systems efficient?	
Are assessments covering appropriate parts of the curriculum?	
Is the teacher following the school assessment policies and practices?	
Are assessments analytical, rather than just descriptive?	
Is assessment information useful? How is it used to inform planning?	
How are the pupils with SEN being monitored against their IEP targets?	
Are appropriate targets being set?	
Is progress towards the children's targets being monitored?	
How accurate is the teacher in judging the National Curriculum level of pieces of work?	
Is marking up to date?	
Are reports well written?	
Do reports give a clear picture of the child?	
How does the teacher keep information for and received from parents' meetings?	

© Sara Bubb 2000

Figure 8.3 Monitoring a teacher's assessment practices

Sampling children's work

Children's work is a useful source of evidence about the effectiveness of an NQT. It is in many ways the proof of the pudding. Again, it is easier to select the work of a few children of different levels of attainment rather than look at the whole class. Figure 8.4 can be used as a format to sample work.

Observation

Observation is a powerful tool for assessing and monitoring a teacher's progress. Used well, it can also be a way to support NQTs, because observation gives such a detailed picture and enables very specific objectives to be set. The value of observation, however, depends on how well it is planned, executed and discussed afterwards (Hagger and McIntyre 1994, p. 10). It is almost always a stressful experience, not only for the teacher but also for the observer. NQTs are used to being observed: they would normally have been watched once every week on teaching practice. During the induction period, however, observation will only happen about once every half term (the TTA recommended minimum) which means that NQTs might feel a greater pressure for it to go well. Look at Activity 8.1 to think about good practice in observation.

Activity 8.1
Remembering what it is like to be observed

Think back to the times you have been observed.
  What happened before the observation and how did you feel?
  What happened during the observation and how did you feel?
  What happened after the observation and how did you feel?
Bearing these experiences in mind, how do you want to go about making the observation and feeding back your findings?

© Sara Bubb 2000

Induction tutors may also find observing stressful, because they feel inexperienced and uncertain of the best way to go about it. The year group and area of the curriculum to be taught may not be familiar. They may feel that their observation and feedback will compare unfavourably to that of the university supervisor whom the NQT has been used to. As the person responsible for the NQT, they will also be mindful of the need to move them forward while maintaining a good relationship. This can lead induction tutors to be too kind, and to not bite the bullet. NQTs sometimes feel that they are not being sufficiently challenged. This is particularly true of the most successful ones, but they too need to be helped to develop professionally.

Observation and giving feedback are very complex skills, for which training and practice are required. The important thing to remember is that the whole process needs to be useful for the NQT. It is for their benefit that it is being done. To this end it is essential that induction tutors consider the context of the observation. This includes:

– the stage of the NQT;
– how they are feeling;
– their previous experiences of being observed;

Prompts for sampling work	Comments
Does the children's work match the teacher's planning?	
Is there a balance of work, e.g. text, sentence and word level in literacy books?	
Is there evidence of the teacher's systems being used, e.g. date, title, handwriting conventions?	
Are school policies in use?	
What does the presentation tell you about the children's motivation and concentration?	
Are children doing enough work? Compare their output with a parallel class.	
How is work differentiated?	
Is there enough challenge for low, average and high attainers so that all can make progress?	
Is there progress over time?	
What difference is there between work at the beginning and end of exercise books or folders?	
Is there any unnecessary repetition?	
Is the work marked in accordance with the school policy?	
Do children know how well they have met the objective of the work?	
Are children responding to the teacher's marking?	
Are errors corrected?	
What systems are there for dealing with repeated errors?	
Is there evidence that children are taking their targets into account?	

© Sara Bubb 2000

Figure 8.4 Sampling children's work

- the state of the induction tutor's relationship with the NQT;
- what part of the school year, week and day it happens in; and
- the disposition of the class.

Induction tutors also need to recognise their own values, beliefs and moods. When I was less experienced I had strong views on what I considered good teaching to be. With hindsight, this was very subjective, narrow and arrogant. This is why it is important to concentrate on the progress the children make before judging the effectiveness of the teaching. The more I observe other teachers, the more convinced I am that there is no one way to teach.

Observers should also recognise their own feelings at the time of the observation. No one functions effectively when they are tired, stressed or irritable. People tend to be more generous and easygoing when feeling happy. Induction tutors must recognise their feelings, and in some way compensate for them, in order to be as objective as possible. They also need to recognise that their very presence in the classroom will affect the children. This is accentuated as the children will know them as another member of staff, perhaps even their former teacher.

Making an observation – points to consider

Before the observation
1. Agree a date and time well in advance. Choose a lesson the NQT feels happy with.
2. Agree how long you will be observing – a whole session is ideal, but this may be too long for the NQT.
3. Ensure that both of you are clear about the purpose of the observation. Let NQTs have a copy of the proforma and criteria you'll be using.
4. Discuss with the NQT what should be the focus of the observation. In the first few weeks this could usefully be classroom organisation, planning, management of the lesson, and very importantly, management of the pupils. Many problems at this stage are to do with easily remedied things, such as organisation of tables. Relate the focus to progress in meeting objectives.
5. Discuss ground rules such as how your presence is to be explained to the class, what you are going to do, where you should sit, your exact time of arrival.
6. Discuss what you will need before or at the beginning of the observation, such as the lesson plan and access to the planning file. If you need something in advance, agree when the NQT is going to give it to you.
7. Agree a time and place to feedback, giving yourself time to reflect and write notes, ideally within 24 hours of the observation.
8. Give the NQT a written copy of the arrangements, to avoid confusion.
9. To build up trust, arrange for the NQT to observe you teach before you watch them.
10. Be positive and optimistic, to aid the NQT's confidence.

Prepare them for feedback by giving them tips such as these:

- Before the feedback, reflect on the lesson yourself in terms of the progress pupils made. What were you pleased with? What could have gone better?
- Listen well. Don't just hear what you want or expect to hear.
- Make notes of salient points.
- Focus on what is being said rather than how it is being said.

- Focus on feedback as information rather than criticism.
- Explain reasons for doing something that might not have been clear to the observer.
- Ask for clarification of anything you are unsure of.
- Try to summarise the main points of the feedback, asking the person who is giving the feedback if they agree.
- Ask for advice and ideas.
- Afterwards, reflect on the feedback. Feel good about the positive comments and think about how to improve.

Choosing an observation format

There is no such thing as an ideal lesson observation proforma, yet sometimes anything seems better than a blank piece of paper. Different formats will be useful at different times. Look at the following list and try Activity 8.2.

1. OFSTED evidence forms (OFSTED 1999) – these may seem too formal and their association not conducive to how the induction tutor wants to be perceived. The seven point grading, however, might be useful in helping you decide whether the teaching and learning was good enough.
2. Chronological notes with 5 minute event sampling – these give a good description of what occurs in a lesson but involve much writing and are not useful for giving the big picture.
3. Detailed checklists of the QTS Standards (see Appendix 1) – these keep one focused on criteria but are lengthy and may not give a flavour of the particular lesson.
4. A sheet with prompts (see Figures 8.5 and 8.6) – this enables you to write freely about what seems useful, but the prompts focus you on areas you need to consider. The prompts could be written beforehand according to the agreed focus of the lesson.
5. A form with sections under the different headings of the Induction Standards, such as Figure 8.7 – the headings will be useful but the size of the boxes may constrain you or make you feel that you are writing something for the sake of it.
6. A strengths and areas for development sheet (see Figure 8.8) – this gives a clear picture of your judgements but needs to be backed up with evidence and examples. Unless you are very experienced, this is best used as a summary sheet after one of the above-mentioned formats has been used.

It is essential to look at teaching in relation to learning. One must always be thinking about cause and effect. Why are the children behaving as they are? The cause is often related to teaching. Thus, the observer needs to look carefully at what both the teacher and the children are doing. Too often the teacher gets most of the attention, yet the product of their work is the children's learning – the proof of the pudding. For note-taking purposes decide whether the main focus is going to be on the pupils and their learning and behaviour (Figure 8.5) with the teaching as the cause, or whether the focus is the teacher with the children's learning and behaviour as the result (Figure 8.6). It can be useful to distinguish between children of different attainment – high attainers (HA), average attainers (AA) and low attainers (LA). At times, one needs to distinguish between children of different sexes or backgrounds.

Activity 8.2

Try out a range of different observation formats, perhaps using a video of some teaching.

Consider the merits and drawbacks of each format.

Which is easiest for you to use?

Which is the most useful?

© Sara Bubb 2000

During the observation

1. Read the lesson plan, paying particular attention to the learning objective. Is it a sensible objective, and is it shared with the children? Annotate the plan, for instance showing what parts went well, when pace slowed, and so forth.
2. If the NQT hasn't given you a place to sit, choose one which is outside the direct line of their vision, but where you can see the children and what the teacher is doing. When the children are doing activities, move around to ascertain the effectiveness of the NQT's explanation, organisation and choice of task. Look at different groups (girls and boys; high, average and low attainers; and children with English as an additional language) to see whether everyone's needs are being met.
3. Look at the NQT's planning file to see what the lesson is building on.
4. Make notes about what actually happens, focusing on the agreed areas but keeping your eyes open to everything. Make clear judgements as you gather evidence.
5. Try to tell the story of the lesson, by noting causes and effect. For instance, what was it about the teacher's delivery that caused children's rapt attention or fidgeting?
6. Refer to the Teaching and Class Management Induction or QTS Standards – have a copy with you.
7. Think about the pupils' learning and what it is about the teaching that is helping or hindering it. Note what children actually achieve. Teachers are not always aware that some children have only managed to write the date and that others have exceeded expectations, for instance. Look through children's books to get a feel for their progress and the teacher's marking.
8. Avoid teaching the children yourself or interfering in any way. This is very tempting! Children will often expect you to help them with spellings, for instance, but once you help one others will ask. This will distract you from your central purpose which is to observe the teaching and learning. It is not wise to intervene in controlling the class unless things get out of hand, because it can undermine the NQT's confidence and may confuse the children, who will see you as the one in charge rather than their teacher. As far as possible be unobtrusive.

Observing Children's Learning

Teacher: **Date and time:**
Subject: **Additional adults:**
Learning objective:
Observer:

Prompts	HA	AA	LA	Comments. What has the teacher done to get this response from the children?
Comply with ground rules.				
Pay attention.				
Behave well.				
Relate well to adults and pupils.				
Are interested.				
Understand what they are to do.				
Understand why they are doing an activity.				
Gain new knowledge and skills.				
Speak and listen well.				
Errors corrected.				
Work hard.				
Act responsibly.				
Understand how well they have done.				
Understand how they can improve.				
Praised for work.				

Figure 8.5 Lesson Observation Sheet – how well children learn

© Sara Bubb 2000

Observing Teaching

Teacher: **Date and time:**
Subject: **Additional adults:**
Learning objective:
Observer:

Prompts	OK?	Comments and evidence. What impact does the teaching have on the children?
Ground rules.		
Praises good behaviour and work.		
Redirects off task behaviour.		
Consequences for poor behaviour.		
High expectations.		
Organised.		
Resources.		
Shares learning objectives.		
Subject knowledge.		
Relates new learning to old.		
Explanations.		
Deals with misunderstandings.		
Voice – tone, volume.		
Pace.		
Use of time.		
Questioning.		
Motivating.		
Differentiation.		
Additional adults.		
Feedback to children.		
Suitable activities.		
Plenary.		

Figure 8.6 Lesson Observation Sheet with teaching prompts

© Sara Bubb 2000

Classroom Observation Form	
NQT:	Subject, date and time:
Observer:	Learning objective:
Additional adults:	Focus of observation:

Planning

Teaching

Class management

Figure 8.7 Classroom Observation Form

Summary of Classroom Observation	
NQT:	Subject, date and time:
Observer:	Focus of observation:

Strengths of the lesson

Areas for further development

Objectives

NQT's signature	Observer's signature

© Sara Bubb 2000

Figure 8.8 Summary of Classroom Observation

9. Remember that as an established member of staff, your presence will normally have an effect on the pupils – they will often be better behaved. It is sometimes useful to leave the room for five minutes and loiter nearby to see if the noise level rises when you are not there and to get a feel for the atmosphere as you go back in. This can also be used when the lesson is going badly because it gives the NQT the opportunity to pull the class together.

10. Look friendly and positive throughout, even (and especially) if things are not going well. Say something positive to the NQT as you leave the class. Ideally, give an indication that you were pleased with what you saw. The NQT will be very anxious, and will almost always think the worst unless reassured.

After the observation

Think about the teaching and learning you have seen, focusing on strengths and a few areas for development. Use the format in Figure 8.8 for writing points to share with the NQT. Be clear about your main message. There is no point listing every little thing that went wrong. You need to have 'the big picture' in order to convey it to the teacher. Remember it needs to be useful to them – aim to help them develop. You want to avoid the extremes of crushing them or giving the impression that things are better than they really are. It is a very fine line to tread, but your knowledge of the context and the NQT will help you.

Ask the NQT how they thought it went, and why. This will give you an insight into how well they can evaluate their work. Be aware of what you say, and how you say it. Try to ask questions to guide their thinking, but not in a way that intimidates or implies criticism. Encourage reflection and listen well by asking open-ended questions, such as:

- How do you think the lesson went?
- What were you most pleased with? Why?
- What did the pupils learn?
- What did the lower attaining pupils learn?
- What did the higher attaining pupils learn?
- Why do you think the lesson went the way it did?
- Were there any surprises?
- When you did . . . . . . the pupils reacted by . . . . . . Why do you think that happened?
- Help me understand what you took into account when you were planning.
- If you taught that lesson again, what, if anything, would you do differently?

Another useful strategy is to use factual statements (Malderez and Bodoczky 1999) about what you heard or saw, without including a judgement. For example, if you say, 'I saw three children yawn during the plenary' the NQT can offer their reason for the behaviour. This enables them to think of explanations, and probably solutions. However, if the observer interprets what was seen as 'I saw three children looking bored' the NQT is immediately put on the defensive and is unlikely to open up and reflect in a confident way.

Be aware of your body language and notice the NQT's. A large proportion of communication is non-verbal, so:

- lean slightly forward;
- uncross arms;

Phase	Mentee action	Mentor action	Mentor style
1. 'Talk me through. . .'	Describes	Listens actively	Non-directive
2. 'I saw. . .'	Listens and interprets	Describes	Collaborative
3. 'How else might you. . .?'	Consider alternatives	Probes	Alternatives
4. 'Why don't you. . .?'	Agrees	Makes decisions, sets tasks	Directive

Figure 8.9 Framework for a feedback session (from Malderez and Bodoczky 1999 *Mentor Courses*, p. 202)

– uncross legs or cross them loosely;
– try to ignore any of your distracting inner thoughts;
– make eye contact;
– smile and nod; and
– listen actively.

Avoid talking about yourself or other teachers you have seen, unless this will be useful to the NQT. It is sometimes tempting to talk about your awful day. This can be comforting for the NQT, but can detract from the purpose of the feedback session. Aim for the NQT to do most of the talking and thinking.

Paraphrase and summarise what the NQT says. This helps the induction tutor concentrate on what is being said and is very helpful in getting a clear shared understanding of what the NQT thinks. It involves reflecting back your interpretation of what you have heard, which can be very useful for the NQT. Use phrases such as 'So what you mean is . . .', 'In other words . . .'.

Be positive and upbeat throughout. Sandwich potentially negative comments between positive ones. Be sensitive to how the NQT is taking your feedback, and ease off if necessary.

Malderez and Bodoczky (1999) suggest using a framework for feedback that has different styles and actions in each of the phases, as is shown in Figure 8.9. I have found that this helps the person feeding back to focus on the main points. It stops one going round in circles or going off on unhelpful tangents. I have adapted this framework (see Figure 8.10) to lead into setting objectives and to end on a positive note by reaffirming the NQT's strengths.

Agree up to three SMART objectives as a result of the observation. Remember that they can be set to develop strengths further, as well as addressing weaknesses. See ideas for setting objectives in Chapter 5.

End on a very encouraging note. Say something to the effect that everyone has similar problems, but that they are easily remedied. Try to convey that you have every faith in the NQT. Give them confidence to carry on. Make sure you give the impression that the NQT is safe in your hands – there is nothing more terrifying than the induction tutor looking worried!

Give a copy of the lesson observation summary notes and objectives set to the NQT as soon as possible, making sure that you too keep a copy just in case theirs gets lost.

Phase initiated by induction tutor	NQT action	Induction tutor action	Induction tutor style
1. 'How do you think it went?' 'Talk me through. . .'	Describes	Listens actively	Non-directive
2. 'I saw. . .'	Listens and interprets	Describes	Collaborative
3. 'How else might you. . .?'	Considers alternatives	Probes	Alternatives
4. 'Why don't you. . .?'	Agrees Thinks of actions	Makes decisions	Directive
5. 'What objectives would help you? What needs to happen?'	Thinks of objectives and action plan	Helps think of objectives and actions. Writes them down	Collaborative and directive
6. 'Finally, I want to remind you that I'm very pleased with. . .'	Listens Feels positive	Summarises reaffirming strengths and progress	Boosting

Figure 8.10 Framework for a feedback session that leads into setting objectives (adapted from Malderez and Bodoczky 1999 *Mentor Courses*, p. 202)

Case study of an observation

Here is an example of an observation and feedback of a reception class teacher from Denis Hayes' *The Handbook for Newly Qualified Teachers – Meeting the Swtandards in Primary and Middle Schools*.

Extract from The Handbook for Newly Qualified Teachers by Denis Hayes

Exercise 1.3 Case study

Read the following extract about the first occasion that Gemma, the NQT, is observed by her induction tutor, and reflect upon the feedback she receives.

Gemma felt nervous. It was the first time that her induction tutor, Sue Danielson, had come to observe her teaching. Not that Gemma was normally nervous. On the contrary, one of the reasons she had been appointed as reception teacher was due to her bouncy disposition and ability to relate to adults, including parents. In fact, unknown to Gemma, the interview panel had agreed that she was the best candidate they had ever interviewed; just right for the job. But now the time had come for the formal part of the appraisal process to begin. Sue would come in for the full morning session, to sit and observe during the literacy hour and be a 'participant observer', taking one of the groups, during maths. Gemma had never really minded being observed as a student, but this was different. Better in some ways; worse in others. It was better because she and Sue has spent a long time discussing things in advance. Sue had stressed the fact that she was only interested in offering help and support, not in finding fault and undermining Gemma's confidence. It was worse because there was a new sense of professional pride involved. Gemma felt slightly irritated that it was necessary for her to 'be observed'. After all, both Sue, the head and just about everyone connected with the school agreed that Gemma had made an excellent start. Parents seemed pleased; the children had settled well and were learning; support staff found Gemma to be a pleasant, responsive and encouraging person. What more did they want? Gemma suppressed a rising sense of indignation. In fact, the session went smoothly, despite Gemma's concerns. It was hard going during the literacy hour which, as usual, turned out to be nearer 45 minutes. The little ones simply could not concentrate for a whole hour and Gemma found it much better to shorten the formal part of the lesson and end on positive note, rather than drag the proceedings out for the sake of conformity. Gemma noted with pleasure that Sue was laughing along with the children at the use of puppets during the interactive phases of the lesson and during the happy song to conclude the lesson. Even the maths lesson went quite well from Gemma's perspective. She struggled with the 'mental maths' introduction, though the children did their best to respond. They seemed a little weary after the literacy and Gemma wondered whether it was really such a good idea for maths to invariably follow literacy, especially for the little children. She would, ideally, have liked to follow up one or two things from before the break and ended the morning with a more practical, collaborative activity, but the timetable was inflexible. By the end of the morning, after the clearing up, hand washing, lining up for meals and dismissal, Sue came across and thanked Gemma warmly. Gemma smiled broadly, but thought that she detected just a hint of incompleteness in Sue's fulsome praise. What had she done? What was Sue going to say? Gemma swallowed hard as this was not likely to be easy, though she may have been a little more reassured had she realised that Sue's heart was pounding too! Sue, aware of Gemma's sensitivity, was anxious to choose her words carefully and get across the fact that although Gemma had done very well, there was still some way to go before her undoubted potential would be fully realised. She hoped desperately that she wouldn't undermine Gemma's confidence, damage their relationship or jeopardise the excellent start that Gemma had made. They had agreed to discuss the issues immediately over lunch, so they headed off for a quiet corner, packed lunches in hand. Gemma was eager to hear the verdict. Sue was equally keen to ensure that in the haste to give feedback, she had got her thinking straight. Both of them were conscious that they had yet to get their resources ready for the afternoon session. They sat down and Sue began by describing the morning session broadly and commenting positively on the children's behaviour and application to their learning. Gemma began to relax. This was sounding positive. Gradually Sue introduced a few quesitons and gently asked Gemma to explain some aspects of the lesson. Gemma did so in her usual direct manner, though she became aware of how defensive she was sounding and became irritated by her own unsettled emotions. Sue nodded, smiled regularly and thanked Gemma for the explanations. Time went by quickly and the half hour flew past. They agreed that Sue would write a summary of her comments and list of the questions she had asked. Gemma would respond in writing and they would further discuss the key issues and establish new targets for the coming weeks.

Sue's commentary on the Literacy Hour

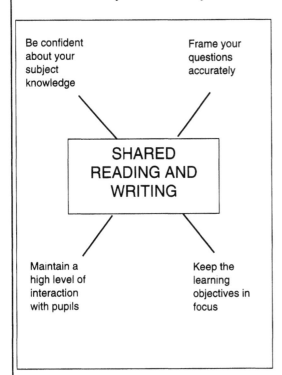

Literacy Hour: Shared reading and writing

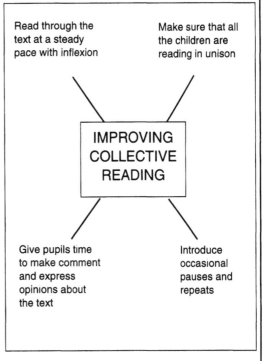

Literacy Hour: Improving collective reading

Lesson plans

Well prepared, fitted well with medium-term plans. Sufficient detail without being over-crowded.

Clarity of intention

Lesson objectives clearly stated. A specific mention of the needs of children with special educational requirements would have enhanced the overall impact.

Introduction

Beautifully done. The use of puppets was excellent and the children were enthralled. Watch for children who call out.

Clarity of explanation to children

Purposeful and using appropriate language. Would it help to use another strategy for ensuring that the children really do understand? For instance, choosing someone to tell the class what had to be done, or pretending to forget what you had just told them and getting the children to remind you?

Purpose of activities

Closely connected with the lesson purpose. I particularly like the sequencing tasks. A few children on independent tasks did not seem altogether clear about what they were expected to do and became a bit restless as a result.

Quality of children's work

As usual with this age, they did not accomplish a lot on paper, but all those with activity sheets seemed to finish them comfortably. I wonder if your brighter children might have something additional to extend them? (I do realise that it is hard to find interesting and relevant things day after day!

Lesson review (plenary)

The best part of the lesson in many ways. You have a wonderful gift for involving the children, drawing in the fringe members and celebrating success.

Conclusion of lesson

Children are learning to tidy up for themselves. You will have to persevere to involve all the children and not just the compliant ones.

Teaching skills

A lovely voice, full of interest and enthusiasm, excellent shading and variety of tone. You maintain excellent eye contact, move purposefully and give the strong impression that you know what you are doing (I'm sure you do!), and that you will stand no nonsense.

Control and discipline

Good throughout. Nearly all the children took turns, engaged with their work and cooperated well. I like the way that you praised the positive aspects of behaviour and were so patient with Paulette when she started getting spiteful. Watch out for some of the 'shadow' children who seem to be working steadily but are furtively wasting time or causing distractions.

Activity 8.3

Having read about the observation and feedback consider:

- Why Gemma was so unsettled by the lesson observation process.
- Your own response to Sue's written feedback (as if you were Gemma).
- How Gemma's progress in teaching compares with your own experience.
- Would you have done the observation and feedback like Sue?

The monitoring of an NQT's progress will inform the end of term assessment meetings and reports on the NQT. This will be the focus of the next chapter.

9 Assessment meetings and reports

Holding formal assessment meetings

The three formal assessment meetings are very important, and useful, in reviewing progress. They should be held towards the end of each term, and are the forum for the termly assessment reports to be discussed and written. They should be seen as significantly different from the ongoing meetings between the NQT and induction tutor because they are a summary of progress so far. Another difference is that the head teacher should attend. Standardised forms (see Appendix 2) have to be filled in and sent to the Appropriate Body (usually the LEA) within 10 days of the meeting. The appropriate body will usually set their own deadlines for reports.

If you have a number of NQTs you will need to be very well organised in order to hold all the assessment meetings before the end of term, particularly the one just before Christmas. Tempting as it may seem, you should not use one meeting to discuss more than one NQT. Each teacher should have their own individual report and assessment meeting. Because of its more formal nature it is worth thinking about assessment meetings carefully. See Activity 9.1.

Activity 9.1

Preparing for a formal assessment meeting

Think about meetings and reports that have focused on your performance.

What did you value or dislike about them?

What can you do to ensure that this meeting is a positive one?

© Sara Bubb 2000

Organising the meeting

Choose the venue carefully and in discussion with the NQT. The TTA recommends,

> The best setting is likely to be one that is conducive to a private professional discussion, where all involved will feel comfortable and where there is very little likelihood of being interrupted or overheard.
> (1999d, p. 11)

Holding the meeting in the NQT's classroom gives them a feeling of control that may not be present in the head teacher's office. It also means that there is easy access to further evidence, such as children's work.

The head teacher should attend the meeting, especially since they will have to sign the assessment form. Most will already have a secure picture of how the NQT is doing, but for some it will be a good opportunity to gain information about the new teacher's progress. This will almost always be of benefit to the NQT. On the other hand, the presence of the head teacher may unnerve them and result in them not speaking up for themselves confidently.

Choose a date that is convenient to all and make sure that at least a week's notice is given. It is ideal if the meeting takes place during the school day, though I am sure that in practice many primary schools will find this hard to organise. Think carefully about a realistic start and finish time. The length of the meeting will depend on the degree of agreement about the NQT's performance and how much preparatory work on the report has been done. A straightforward case, where the participants are well briefed, should take not much more than half an hour. An agenda such as the one in Figure 9.1 will help all to know the focus of different parts of the meeting, and formalises the meeting.

INDUCTION PERIOD – TERM 1
Assessment meeting between NQT, induction tutor and head teacher
10 December 4.00–5.00 pm
Venue: NQT's classroom

Agenda

1. Clarification of purpose of meeting.
2. Assessment of Planning, Teaching and Class Management.
3. Assessment of Monitoring, Assessment, Recording, Reporting and Accountability.
4. Assessment of Other Professional Requirements.
5. Read and amend the draft assessment report form. NQT to make written comment during or after the meeting.
6. Review the present induction provision and plan the future support and monitoring that will enable the NQT to meet their new objectives.

Figure 9.1 Sample agenda for the first assessment meeting (adapted from TTA 1999 *Supporting Induction for Newly Qualified Teachers. Part 3: Assessment*, p. 12)

Evidence to inform the assessment meeting

It is essential that the assessment meeting is based on hard evidence. This may take various forms, such as:

- records of observations – there should be at least two a term and ideally not all made by the same person;
- records from meetings with the induction tutor;
- self-assessment by the NQT;
- the diary sheets from the school based induction programme;
- notes from a centrally organised induction programme, if one is attended;
- analysis of pupils' work and assessment records, both formal and informal;
- monitored samples of the NQT's planning and lesson evaluations;
- information about the NQT's liaison with others SENCO, parents and colleagues.

It is not necessary to collect large amounts of supporting evidence – filling in the formats in this book will be sufficient. It is more helpful to select specific pieces of evidence that arise from the NQT's day-to-day work, and from the induction monitoring and support programme, to illustrate progress and achievement in relation to the Induction Standards.

Writing the report

The report form suggested by the DfEE in Circular 5/99 consists of three A4 pages (see Appendix 2). The first page consists of information about the NQT and school, and some tick boxes; the second requires the induction tutor to write under the three Induction Standard headings; and the third is for the NQT to comment, and for all involved to sign.

Completing the first page of the report

Formal reports have to be completed at the end of each term. The form for the first and second terms requires the head teacher to tick one of two statements:

> The above named teacher's progress indicates that he/she will be able to meet the requirements for the satisfactory completion of the induction period.

> The above named teacher is not making satisfactory progress towards the requirements for the satisfactory completion of the induction period.

> (DfEE 1999, Annex B)

Deciding which box to tick will be straightforward in the majority of cases. However, many induction tutors would like some intermediate statement because they are concerned about their NQT's performance but would not go so far as to say that it was unsatisfactory. One has to balance professional honesty with the need to keep the NQT boosted enough to try to improve. Also bear in mind that the assessment forms are sent to the Appropriate Body, who need to be alerted to any weak NQTs so that they can take appropriate action. A useful rule of thumb is that if more than one in ten lessons is unsatisfactory, using the OFSTED criteria, the NQT is not making satisfactory progress. Remember the children. Those in an NQT's class are just as entitled to a good education as the children in an experienced teacher's class.

The head teacher must also tick the kinds of monitoring and support that have been in place during the term. These are:

> Observations of the NQT's teaching and provision of feedback.

> Discussions between the NQT and the induction tutor to review progress and set objectives.

> Observations of experienced teachers by the NQT.

> An assessment meeting between the NQT and the induction tutor.

> (DfEE 1999, Annex B)

All should be ticked if the school is supporting the NQT well, and any omissions will alert the appropriate body that things are not happening as they should.

Completing the second page of the report – about the Induction Standards

The bulk of the report involves writing briefly under three headings about the extent to which the NQT is meeting the Standards. In areas where the NQT is not considered to have made satisfactory progress, weaknesses should be clearly outlined with evidence. Objectives for the following term should be set and the support planned.

How to go about writing the report

1. Read the QTS and Induction Standards to refresh your memory. These are the criteria that need to be commented on, though not every standard needs to be mentioned.
2. For the end of term assessment use the summary notes in Figure 9.2 to consider the NQT's strengths and areas for development under the headings of the Standards. If there are issues around knowledge and understanding – and there undoubtedly will be – put them either in the section on Planning, Teaching and Class Management or Other Professional Requirements.
3. Ask the NQT to do a self-evaluation using the same strengths and areas for development format in Figure 9.2. This reflection will be very useful for both of you. Comparing notes will give you an up-to-date and often very detailed picture of the NQT. Be aware, however, that the majority of NQTs have very high expectations of themselves and will consider some things weaknesses that are perfectly fine.
4. Decide what you think are the main issues. If there are weaknesses, diagnose the root of the problem and focus on that.
5. Select the main points and either type or write them by hand in draft. See it as a working document that can be typed up after the meeting and when the NQT has had time to write a response. Share this with the NQT, ideally a little before the assessment meeting so that they have time to respond.
6. Write the report *about*, not *to* the NQT. Adopt a formal style.
7. Be positive – we can cope with criticism if our good points are celebrated. Be effusive in praising strengths, but make sure your message is clear, especially where there are areas of weakness.
8. If space allows, refer briefly to the evidence for your judgements. Certainly make sure you have evidence to hand at the assessment meeting. Ideally, there will be no surprises if points have been raised throughout the term.
9. Try to be objective – celebrate strengths but do not duck weaknesses. If you are worried about anything you must say so. Do not avoid issues in the hope that the NQT will remedy them in time – they may turn into a bigger problem. Always bear the worst case scenario in mind: your report may be part of the evidence in a future appeal.
10. Have some thoughts about what objectives to set, and how to phrase them. They can be written at the end of the meeting, in collaboration with the head teacher and NQT.
11. During the meeting, be prepared to add or revise the wording of the assessment. NQTs will feel justifiably aggrieved if they feel that the only input they have into the report is completing the box for their comment.
12. Give the document with revisions to the NQT for their optional written comment.

Assessment Summary Notes

Date: **NQT:**   **Induction tutor:**

Planning, Teaching and Class Management – Strengths:	Planning, Teaching and Class Management – Areas for development:
Monitoring, Assessment, Recording, Reporting and Accountability – Strengths:	Monitoring, Assessment, Recording, Reporting and Accountability – Areas for development:
Other Professional Requirements – Strengths:	Other Professional Requirements – Areas for development:

Figure 9.2 Summary notes for the end of term assessment – to be used by the induction tutor and as a form of self-evaluation by the NQT

Encourage them to make a comment. They should be proactive throughout the induction process as well as demonstrating that they are reflective about their own practice.

13. Ask the secretary to type up the finished document. Check it for errors – spelling mistakes are so embarrassing! Ask the head teacher, induction tutor and NQT to sign it. Give everyone copies, and send a copy to the LEA within 10 days of the meeting.

Styles of writing

It is very useful to look at other people's reports to get ideas about style and useful phrases. Compare what has been written about some fictional successful NQTs, Riffat, Keith and Theresa, with the sections about Tony (TTA 1999d) who is doing less well, particularly in Planning, Teaching and Class Management. Activity 9.2 will help you do this. Notice how one normally needs to write more when progress has not been satisfactory.

Activity 9.2
Analysing reports

Compare the writing styles of the reports on the different NQTs (see Examples below).

What do you like about the way these NQTs have been written about?

Is there anything you do not like about the way these NQTs have been written about?

Examine two sentences that you think are well phrased. What is it that you like about them?

Do you feel that the reports are sufficiently addressing the nub of the Standards?

© Sara Bubb 2000

Planning, Teaching and Class Management

Example 1: Riffat (nursery)
Riffat is making good progress in all areas. Observations of Riffat's teaching show that she is able to plan to meet the needs of children of all abilities and is also able to plan for children with EAL and SEN. She makes a good contribution to medium and long-term planning, and produces detailed and effective plans for key activities.

She understands and is effective in her role as a key worker and has built excellent relationships with her focus children and their families.

Riffat has adapted quickly to the complicated rota and routine of the school and puts all policies into practice. Riffat implements the school's behaviour policy and has developed effective strategies for managing the behaviour of individuals and large groups.

Riffat's teaching shows she has sound expectations and a regard for equal opportunities.

© Sara Bubb 2000

Example 2: Keith

Keith is making good progress. He plans effectively and has followed the planning policy of the school. He works in partnership with the other year group teacher. He identifies appropriate teaching objectives and specifies clearly how they will be taught. He sets relevant, demanding tasks for the children and has been observed using effective teaching strategies for the whole class, groups and individuals. His planning is also clearly differentiated to meet the needs of the pupils. The standard of behaviour of the pupils is high, with appropriate rules and expectations well established. The school's behaviour policy is followed. The classroom itself is tidy, well organised and is a stimulating learning environment which communicates enthusiasm for what is being taught.

There are a number of children in the class on the SEN register, including one with a statement. Current IEPs are in place and, in consultation with the SENCO, clear targets have been set, and these are referred to when planning. There is also regular collection of evidence to monitor progress.

Example 3: Tony (TTA 1999d, p. 28)

Tony is making satisfactory progress in some areas, but not in others.

Observations of Tony's teaching show that he has built excellent relationships with his pupils. Their behaviour is generally good and Tony handles inappropriate behaviour well.

Tony makes good use of the school's long and medium-term planning frameworks, but pupils' work suggests that his short-term planning for specific classes continues to be insufficiently focused on improving his pupils' achievement. There is little differentiation and Tony tends to focus his teaching on the more able pupils, accepting underachievement too readily. In his self-evaluation Tony recognises his continuing difficulty in adapting his planning and teaching to provide an appropriate range of activities. He needs to make considerable progress in this aspect of his teaching in order to meet the induction requirements.

In the second term, Tony has agreed to renew the objective of developing his ability to set appropriate learning objectives for *all* of his pupils and using these as a basis for his planning and teaching. He will aim to develop his mathematics teaching further, but has also agreed a new objective relating to raising his expectations of pupil achievement in literacy. (Copy of the relevant page from section C of the CEP is attached.)

Tony has found it particularly useful to observe the practice of other teachers in this and another school, and this will be a key element of his support this term. Further support will also be provided by Tony's induction tutor and by the school's literacy and mathematics coordinators.

Monitoring, Assessment, Recording, Reporting and Accountability

Example 1: Riffat (nursery)
Riffat's practice in this area is exemplary. Her assessments are of a very high quality and she monitors her observations to ensure children have been observed in all curriculum areas. Her records are extremely well kept and have been used as an example of good practice for staff and visitors. Riffat has tackled writing reports for the first time and was able to successfully summarise observations from other staff to give accurate portraits of her focus children. Because Riffat's records and assessments were so good she was able to report accurately and effectively at parents' evening.

Example 2: Keith
Keith is making satisfactory progress in this area. He is now very reflective about his teaching and the strengths and weaknesses of individual pupils. He uses a variety of assessment methods including structured observations, testing and marking. He now completes his analysis of these systematically and uses the records to inform his planning. Keith is beginning to set specific targets for individuals and groups in literacy and to use those to make purposeful interventions in learning. With the help of the parallel class teacher, he is also beginning to analyse results, looking for trends to check whether his pupils are making progress against attainment targets. Keith has participated in one formal parents'/carers' meeting successfully and has made himself available to discuss appropriate targets and give advice regarding support at home.

Example 3: Tony (TTA 1999d, p. 28)
Tony is making satisfactory progress in this area.

Observations of Tony's teaching, along with samples of pupils' work and Tony's marking indicate that he is able to make accurate and independent assessments, using the KS2 attainment targets. He has been able to provide detailed and accurate feedback to parents.

Tony could usefully develop his day-to-day monitoring of pupils' achievements and the way in which he uses this in his planning. He also needs to think about how he uses feedback to parents to involve them in their children's learning. Tony has set longer-term objectives in relation to these points. (Copy of the relevant page from section C of the CEP is attached.)

Other Professional Requirements

Example 1: Theresa
Theresa is responsible for one support staff member and a number of parents/carers who have volunteered to work in the room. She is trialling a new school initiative to formalise communications with these people and is recording learning intentions and objectives for the children that the additional adult works with.

Theresa has read the school's policies and has implemented many of them well She seeks support to address incidences of bullying to show both children and parent/carers how seriously she takes them.

Theresa willingly participates in school based INSET and is able to discuss developments taking place in education. She writes reflective notes after attending induction sessions at the professional development centre.

Example 2: Riffat
Riffat behaves in a professional manner at school. She is always punctual, works well as part of the team and has established effective working relationships with all staff members. She is a committed and reflective practitioner who has made an active and constructive contribution to her own professional development. She often draws colleagues' attention to useful articles.

Example 3: Tony (TTA 1999d, p. 28)
Tony is making satisfactory progress in this area.

Observations of Tony in the classroom indicate that support staff are used well to support classroom management. Tony now needs to use their experience and expertise to the full in his planning and the management of children's learning. He has successfully implemented, and contributed to the development of, the school's long-term curriculum plans.

Tony has made an active and constructive contribution to his own professional development and has worked closely with his induction tutor to identify where he is experiencing difficulties, set new objectives and agree appropriate development activities.

© Sara Bubb 2000

The third page of the report – the NQT's comment

NQTs can choose whether or not to make a comment on the report, and are given a box in which to write. I think they should be encouraged to do so since the whole emphasis in induction is on NQTs being proactive and reflective. Some NQTs say which parts of their induction programme have been most useful; others defend themselves; others write about what they feel are their strengths and areas for development. Here are some examples.

Examples of NQTs' comments

Example 1: Keith
During the first term I developed good positive relationships with children and learning support staff in my class. I have developed good displays of children's work and I have good management and control of the class.

Areas to Develop: My learning objectives need to be more tightly focused for each lesson and I need to set and continually update group targets for children's reading and writing. I need to ensure that independent work during mathematics and English lessons can be accomplished by children without teacher support.

Example 2: Sarah
I feel that my progress during the term has been disappointing. I have had problems with control and this has affected my health and self-confidence. My induction tutor has been supportive but has not been able to give me the help I needed because of her other commitments. I feel that the objectives she set for me were not very useful and distracted me from sorting out the behaviour of the class. I was not allowed to go on the LEA induction programme session on behaviour management because there was no one to cover my class.

Example 3: Patsy
I disagree with the report. I have been told that my planning is not satisfactory. This is the first time in a whole term that this has been mentioned. My planning, which is deemed to be unsatisfactory, is as good as the parallel class teacher's. I don't know how I can be expected to teach well when there are practically no schemes of work or resources in the school. My induction tutor has only met with me twice in the whole term. She observed me once, but that was at short notice, and she did not give me any written feedback. She mentioned nothing about weak planning. I do not feel that I am getting the right level of support as an NQT.

© Sara Bubb 2000

Weak NQTs

If an NQT is not making satisfactory progress, the school should set up the monitoring and support that will enable the NQT to improve. There is an expectation in the TTA induction literature that schools should do all they can to help weak NQTs meet the Induction Standards. Early identification is essential – problems do not normally go away without some attention. The TTA recommends that schools contact the LEA as soon as there is a serious concern that has not been resolved through the school's efforts. Schools should not wait until the formal assessment meetings. For more about how to support NQTs with problems see Chapter 9.

Similarly, if NQTs feel that they are not receiving appropriate monitoring and support they should raise their concerns initially with the school and then with the 'named person' that every LEA must appoint as a contact for induction issues. In many LEAs this is someone outside the support, monitoring and assessment roles, perhaps from the personnel department. They will give advice and try to address concerns.

The final assessment report

The final assessment report is different from the reports made at the end of the first and second terms. If you believe that the NQT 'has met the requirements for the satisfactory completion of the induction period' (DfEE 1999, Annex B), the head teacher simply needs to complete the Induction Summary Statement. This does not require any writing to the Standards' headings because it just requires boxes to be ticked. Easy!

If the school decides that the NQT has not met the Induction Standards, a form entitled 'Failure to complete the induction period satisfactorily' (DfEE 1999, Annex B), needs to be completed. This requires writing under each of the three headings. The head teacher must detail:

- Where the Induction Standards have been met.
- Areas of weakness in Standards that have not been met.
- The evidence used to inform the judgement.

In the cases of either a successful or a failing NQT, the head teacher is only making a recommendation to the Appropriate Body (usually the LEA). It is up to them to make the final decision. In the case of failures, many LEAs will want to observe the NQT, but this is not statutory. The LEA is responsible for making sure that the assessment of the NQT was accurate and reliable, that the NQT's objectives were set appropriately and that they were supported. LEAs can grant extensions to the induction period but only in exceptional circumstances. These are where:

> for reasons unforeseen and/or beyond the control of one or more of the parties involved, it is unreasonable to expect the NQT to meet the requirements by the end of the induction period; or
>
> there is insufficient evidence on which a decision can be made about whether the induction requirements have been met. (DfEE 1999, para. 15)

NQTs can appeal to the Secretary of State, or the General Teaching Council when it takes over this role, against the appropriate body's decisions to extend the induction period or fail them. Appeals will be considered by a Teacher Induction Appeal Committe (TIAC) of four people. The appeal procedures are set out in Annex D of Circular 5/99.

The procedures for assessment meetings and reports need to be clear, and ideally part of a school policy that links to performance management and appraisal. The last chapter of this book focuses on developing a school induction policy. This will be very helpful to all concerned, but particularly to the induction tutor. It will ensure that roles, responsibilities and procedures are thought through for an individual school.

10 Developing a school policy for induction

The need for a policy

Schools should have a policy for induction, to ensure fair and consistent treatment of NQTs. When NQTs are not treated well they often feel ambivalent about making a fuss. As two said,

> 'At the end of the day, no matter what structures are in place, it is actually very difficult to discuss problems. I want to pass my induction year and if this means keeping my head down and mouth shut that's what I'll do. The alternative is to highlight problems with my support and then have to face awkward times with my induction tutor or Head, with the implications that might have on whether they pass or fail me.'

> 'Complaining that you are being observed at an inappropriate time or that you have been given little warning simply allows the Head to argue that you are "insecure" about your practice in the classroom.'

The following are complaints that some NQTs have had after one term under statutory induction, some of which could usefully be addressed at a whole-school level or in a policy.

- *Contracts*
  - not being given a written contract or job description;
  - being given a temporary contract;
  - not being given the fair number of points on the salary scale;
  - accepting a job without realising that the above would be issues.
- *10% release time*
  - not getting it;
  - not timetabled until the second term;
  - given at inconvenient times, e.g. in two one hour slots;
  - always given at different times, making it hard to plan;
  - timing is inflexible, so NQT is only able to see certain subjects being taught;
  - cancelled frequently.
- *Induction tutor*
  - hasn't time to do the job;
  - not experienced in the NQT's key stage;
  - not planning how the induction release time should be spent – leaving it up to the NQT.

- *Being observed*
  - not being observed;
  - being observed too often;
  - being observed without warning;
  - being observed at an inappropriate time, e.g. just before Christmas;
  - feedback given too long after the lesson to be of use.
- *Lack of resources*
  - these lead to NQTs being frustrated in their teaching; for instance not having enough basic resources such as reading books for the children to use in class, let alone to take home;
  - NQTs spending their own money on resources; one NQT spent £300 on basics in the first term when she could ill afford to;
  - restricted use of the photocopier makes things worse.
- *Given a very difficult class*
  - NQTs given classes that would challenge an experienced teacher;
  - classes with a high proportion (half the class) of pupils with special needs, including ones with statements;
  - not being helped with SEN because SENCO is on sick leave.
- *Classroom assistants*
  - given the worst in the school;
  - given several, 'I have six support assistants, three of whom are only in the class for 30 minutes a week';
  - coping when they are on sick leave;
  - planning for them, but they don't turn up.
- *Little support with planning*
  - the school is one form entry;
  - the parallel class teachers are on supply and are not interested in team planning;
  - the NQT has to lead the planning because the parallel class teachers are weak, 'they don't even know what an objective is!';
  - NQT's ideas not listened to in planning meetings.
- *Feedback on progress*
  - not given any;
  - too generous – NQT knows she should be doing better but the induction tutor says things are fine;
  - given contradictory advice;
  - too negative;
  - 'Rigid and unrealistic expectations about what I can do, e.g. in the first term the induction tutor expected all assessments to have been made, all forward planning done, all targets monitored, all books marked, and all displays perfect. I feel that I'm always behind and that nothing is done well enough.'

Now look at Activity 10.1.

Activity 10.1

Do you think the complaints listed above would ever be said by NQTs in your school?

How could you ensure that NQTs felt fairly treated?

How would school-wide policies help?

What do you think should be in a school policy for induction?

What the policy might contain

The following provides an outline of the possible content and structures of a school policy on induction.

A. Roles and responsibilities of the head teacher – adapt the TTA's wording to fit your own situation.

B. Roles and responsibilities of the induction tutor – adapt the TTA's wording to fit your own situation. It will be particularly important to consider how the induction tutor will have time and gain the skills to do the job or to outline the people who are taking different parts of the induction tutor's role.

C. Roles and responsibilities of the 'buddy mentor', planning partner, etc.

D. Roles and responsibilities of the NQT – adapt the TTA's wording to fit your own situation.

E. Information on how the following elements of the NQT's entitlement are going to be met:

1. A job description that does not make 'unreasonable' demands.
2. A contract.
3. A fair share of resources (human and material) to enable them to teach effectively.
4. An induction tutor.
5. Meetings with the induction tutor.
6. Support from other staff, particularly with planning, assessment and SEN.
7. The Career Entry Profile (CEP) discussed by NQT and induction tutor.
8. Objectives, informed by the strengths and areas for development identified in the CEP, to help NQTs improve so that they meet the Standards for the induction period.
9. A 10 per cent reduction in timetable.
10. A planned programme of how to spend that time, such as observations of other teachers and attendance on a LEA or university organised induction course.
11. At least one observation each half term, with oral and written feedback.
12. An assessment meeting and report at the end of each term.
13. Procedures for the NQT to air grievances about induction provision at school and a 'named person' to contact at the LEA.

Kevan Bleach has written a policy for his secondary school that concludes with an NQT statement of entitlement (see Figure 10.1). This may give you ideas about the format, content and style of your school policy.

Sneyd Community School

At Sneyd Community School we aim to provide all Newly Qualified Teachers (NQTs) with the opportunity to:

- Gain experience of working with children in the classroom and general school situation.
- Gain experience of school and faculty organisation.
- Observe experienced teachers at work.
- Gain experience in the teaching of individual pupils, groups of pupils and classes.
- Develop essential confidence and the capacity to establish a learning environment.
- Develop skill and understanding in the area of classroom management and control.
- Demonstrate the ability to work harmoniously with children and professional colleagues.
- Gain experience in the planning, execution and evaluation of individual lessons and schemes of work.
- Develop sound and competent teaching strategies.
- Provide a commitment to teaching and ensure that the right choice of career has been made.

To these ends, we pledge to offer NQTs the following commitments

- A year-long period of induction as a condition in the contract of employment.
- The provision of a teaching load that represents no more than 90% of the teaching timetable of an MPG teacher and the protection of all non-contact periods (where possible) in the first term. The provision of a timetable that will offer teaching experience across a range of age and ability.
- Formal lesson observation by the Subject Mentor at least once every half term, according to shared criteria and descriptors, with a written appraisal forming the basis of prompt follow-up discussion and objective-setting.
- Monthly review meetings with the Subject Mentor that focus on the NQT's progress within the context of the QTS and Induction Standards and Objectives identified in the Career Entry Profile (CEP).
- A meeting with the Induction Manager every half term to discuss their progress with Objectives identified in the CEP and to set future Objectives, to formulate their own perspectives on teaching and learning, and to develop an extended professional view of educational issues.
- A meeting with the Induction Manager every term to discuss the content of the NQT's summative assessment report.
- To carry out an audit of each NQT's competence and needs in order to plan relevant and differentiated INSET during induction.
- To enable NQTs to observe teaching by more experienced colleagues.
- To organise observations in partner primary and secondary schools.
- To use funds delegated by the LEA for NQT induction to finance supply cover for suitable courses and observations, professional development materials, etc.
- To offer a professional development continuum into the second year of teaching.

In reciprocation, we hold the following expectations of NQTs

- To take the initiative in seeking advice and help from the Subject Mentor and Induction Manager with any matters relating to their personal and professional welfare.
- To be thoroughly prepared for teaching lessons and to have lesson plans readily available and up-to-date.
- To act upon the constructive comments of staff who observe and advise about teaching and learning.
- To know and use the Induction Standards in monitoring their own work.
- To observe more experienced teachers in the home faculty, elsewhere in the school and on visits to other schools, in order to learn from their established good practice.
- To take full advantage of the school's induction programme.
- To use their Career Entry Profiles for setting objectives for professional development.
- To engage in reflective self-analyses of their professional practice and the underlying assumptions on which they are based.
- To play an active part in the everyday life of the school by fulfilling administrative and pastoral responsibilities and school duties.
- To help maintain the school's professional ethos in terms of appearance and conduct.

Figure 10.1 Excerpt from the Sneyd Community School induction policy by Kevan Bleach

Appendix 1 Standards for the Award of Qualified Teacher Status (DfEE Circular 4/98)

A. KNOWLEDGE AND UNDERSTANDING

1. Secondary

Those to be awarded QTS must, when assessed, demonstrate that they:

a. have a secure knowledge and understanding of the concepts and skills in their specialist subject(s) at a standard equivalent to degree level to enable them to teach it (them) confidently and accurately at:

    i.   KS3 for trainees on 7–14 courses;

    ii. KS3 and KS4 and, where relevant, post-16 for trainees on 11–16 or 18 courses; and

    iii. KS4 and post-16 for trainees on 14–19 courses;

b. **for English, mathematics or science specialists,** have a secure knowledge and understanding of the subject content specified in the relevant Initial Teacher Training National Curriculum[1];

c. have, for their specialist subject(s), where applicable, a detailed knowledge and understanding of the National Curriculum programmes of study, level descriptions or end of key stage descriptions for KS3 and, where applicable, National Curriculum programmes of study for KS4;

d. for Religious Education (RE) specialists, have a detailed knowledge of the Model Syllabuses for RE;

e. are familiar, for their specialist subject(s), with the relevant KS4 and post-16 examination syllabuses and courses, including vocational courses;

f. understand, for their specialist subject(s), the framework of 14–19 qualifications and the routes of progression through it[2];

g. understand, for their specialist subject(s), progression from the KS2 programmes of study[3];

h. know and can teach the key skills required for current qualifications relevant to their specialist subject(s), for pupils aged 14–19, and understand the contribution that their specialist subject(s) make(s) to the development of the key skills[2];

i. cope securely with subject-related questions which pupils raise;

---

1 This does not apply until September 1999.
2 This does not apply to trainees on 7–14 courses.
3 This does not apply to trainees on 14–19 courses.

j. are aware of, and know how to access, recent inspection evidence and classroom-relevant research evidence on teaching secondary pupils in their specialist subject(s), and know how to use this to inform and improve their teaching;

k. know, for their specialist subject(s), pupils' most common misconceptions and mistakes;

l. understand how pupils' learning in the subject is affected by their physical, intellectual, emotional and social development;

m. have, for their specialist subject(s), a secure knowledge and understanding of the content specified in the ITT National Curriculum for Information and Communications Technology in subject teaching;

n. are familiar with subject-specific health and safety requirements, where relevant, and plan lessons to avoid potential hazards.

2. Primary

For all courses those to be awarded QTS must, when assessed, demonstrate that they:

a. understand the purposes, scope, structure and balance of the National Curriculum Orders as a whole and, within them, the place and scope of the primary phase, the key stages, the primary core and foundation subjects and RE;

b. are aware of the breadth of content covered by the pupils' National Curriculum across the primary core and foundation subjects and RE;

c. understand how pupils' learning is affected by their physical, intellectual, emotional and social development.

d. **for each core and specialist subject**[4] covered in their training:

   i.   have, where applicable, a detailed knowledge and understanding of the relevant National Curriculum programmes of study and level descriptions or end of key stage descriptions across the primary age range;

   ii. for RE specialists, have a detailed knowledge of the Model Syllabuses for RE;

   iii. cope securely with subject-related questions which pupils raise;

   iv. understand the progression from SCAA's *Desirable Outcomes for Children's Learning on Entering Compulsory Education* to KS1, the progression from KS1 to KS2, and from KS2 to KS3;

   v.   are aware of, and know how to access, recent inspection evidence and classroom relevant research evidence on teaching primary pupils in the subject, and know how to use this to inform and improve their teaching;

   vi, know pupils' most common misconceptions and mistakes in the subject;

   vii. have a secure knowledge and understanding of the content specified in the ITT National Curriculum for Information and Communications Technology in subject teaching;

   viii. are familiar with subject-specific health and safety requirements, where relevant, and plan lessons to avoid potential hazards;

4 A specialist subject may be one of the core subjects.

e. **for English, mathematics and science,** have a secure knowledge and understanding of the subject content specified in the ITT National Curricula for primary English, mathematics and science[5];

f. **for any specialist subject(s),** have a secure knowledge of the subject to at least a standard approximating to GCE Advanced level in those aspects of the subject taught at KS1 and KS2;

g. **for any non-core, non-specialist subject covered in their training,** have a secure knowledge to a standard equivalent to at least level 7 of the pupils' National Curriculum. For RE, the required standard for non-specialist training is broadly equivalent to the end of key stage statements for Key Stage 4 in QCA's Model Syllabuses for RE[6].

3. **Additional Standards relating to early years (nursery and reception) for trainees on 3–8 and 3–11 courses**

Those to be awarded QTS must, when assessed, demonstrate that they:

a. have a detailed knowledge of SCAA's *Desirable Outcomes for Children's Learning on Entering Compulsory Education*;

b. have a knowledge of effective ways of working with parents and other carers;

c. have an understanding of the roles and responsibilities of other agencies with responsibility for the care of young children.

B. PLANNING, TEACHING AND CLASS MANAGEMENT

This section details the Standards which all those to be awarded QTS must demonstrate, when assessed, in each subject that they have been trained to teach. For primary non-core, non-specialist subjects, trainees being assessed for QTS must meet the required Standards but with the support, if necessary, of a teacher experienced in the subject concerned.

1. **Primary English, mathematics and science**

For all courses, those to be awarded QTS must, when assessed, demonstrate that they:

a. have a secure knowledge and understanding of, and know how and when to apply, the teaching and assessment methods specified in the ITT National Curricula for primary English, mathematics and science[5];

b. have a secure knowledge and understanding of, and know when to apply in relation to each subject, the teaching and assessment methods specified in the ITT National Curriculum for Information and Communications Technology in subject teaching.

---

4   For primary science this does not apply until September 1999.

5, 6   Where providers offer more limited coverage of subjects than the required non-core, non-specialist subjects, **e.g. a few hours of taster training in a foundation subject, safety training in PE and/or design and technology,** the nature and extent of such training can be recorded on the newly qualified teacher's TTA Career Entry Profile.

2. Primary and secondary specialist subjects

For all courses, those to be awarded QTS must, when assessed, demonstrate that they have a secure knowledge and understanding of, and know how and when to apply, in relation to their specialist subject(s), the teaching and assessment methods specified in the ITT National Curriculum for Information and Communications Technology in subject teaching.

3. Secondary English, mathematics and science

To be awarded QTS specialists in secondary English, mathematics or science must, when assessed, demonstrate that they have a secure knowledge and understanding of, and know how and when to apply, the teaching and assessment methods specified in the relevant ITT National Curriculum[1].

4. Primary and secondary for all subjects

Planning

For all courses, those to be awarded QTS must, when assessed, demonstrate that they:

a. plan their teaching to achieve progression in pupils' learning through:

   i. identifying clear teaching objectives and content, appropriate to the subject matter and the pupils being taught, and specifying how these will be taught and assessed;

   ii. setting tasks for whole class, individual and group work, including homework, which challenge pupils and ensure high levels of pupil interest;

   iii. setting appropriate and demanding expectations for pupils' learning, motivation and presentation of work;

   iv. setting clear objectives for pupils' learning, building on prior attainment, and ensuring that pupils are aware of the substance and purpose of what they are asked to do;

   v. identifying pupils who:

- have special educational needs, including specific learning difficulties;
- are very able;
- are not yet fluent in English;

   and knowing where to get help in order to give positive and targeted support;

b. provide clear structures for lessons, and for sequences of lessons, in the short, medium and longer term, which maintain pace, motivation and challenge for pupils;

c. make effective use of assessment information on pupils' attainment and progress in their teaching and in planning future lessons and sequences of lessons;

d. plan opportunities to contribute to pupils' personal, spiritual, moral, social and cultural development;

e. where applicable, ensure coverage of the relevant examination syllabuses and National Curriculum programmes of study.

Teaching and Class Management

For all courses, those to be awarded QTS must, when assessed, demonstrate that they:

f. ensure effective teaching of whole classes, and of groups and individuals within the whole class setting, so that teaching objectives are met, and best use is made of available teaching time;

g. monitor and intervene when teaching to ensure sound learning and discipline;

h. establish and maintain a purposeful working atmosphere;

i. set high expectations for pupils' behaviour, establishing and maintaining a good standard of discipline through well focused teaching and through positive and productive relationships;

j. establish a safe environment which supports learning and in which pupils feel secure and confident;

k. use teaching methods which sustain the momentum of pupils' work and keep all pupils engaged through:

    i. stimulating intellectual curiosity, communicating enthusiasm for the subject being taught, fostering pupils' enthusiasm and maintaining pupils' motivation;

    ii. matching the approaches used to the subject matter and the pupils being taught;

    iii. structuring information well, including outlining content and aims, signalling transitions and summarising key points as the lesson progresses;

    iv. clear presentation of content around a set of key ideas, using appropriate subject-specific vocabulary and well chosen illustrations and examples;

    v. clear instruction and demonstration, and accurate well-paced explanation;

    vi. effective questioning which matches the pace and direction of the lesson and ensures that pupils take part;

    vii. careful attention to pupils' errors and misconceptions, and helping to remedy them;

    viii. listening carefully to pupils, analysing their responses and responding constructively in order to take pupils' learning forward;

    ix. selecting and making good use of textbooks, ICT and other learning resources which enable teaching objectives to be met;

    x. providing opportunities for pupils to consolidate their knowledge and maximising opportunities, both in the classroom and through setting well-focused homework, to reinforce and develop what has been learnt;

    xi. exploiting opportunities to improve pupils' basic skills in literacy, numeracy and ICT, and the individual and collaborative study skills needed for effective learning, including information retrieval from libraries, texts and other sources;

    xii. exploiting opportunities to contribute to the quality of pupils' wider educational development, including their personal, spiritual, moral, social and cultural development;

    xiii. setting high expectations for all pupils notwithstanding individual differences, including gender, and cultural and linguistic backgrounds;

xiv. providing opportunities to develop pupils' wider understanding by relating their learning to real and work-related examples;

l. are familiar with the Code of Practice on the identification and assessment of special educational needs and, as part of their responsibilities under the Code, implement and keep records on individual education plans (IEPs) for pupils at stage 2 of the Code and above;

m. ensure that pupils acquire and consolidate knowledge, skills and understanding in the subject;

n. evaluate their own teaching critically and use this to improve their effectiveness.

5. Additional Standards relating to early years (nursery and reception) for trainees on 3–8 and 3–11 courses

For all courses, those to be awarded QTS must, when assessed, demonstrate that they:

a. plan activities which take account of pupils' needs and their developing physical, intellectual, emotional and social abilities, and which engage their interest;

b. provide structured learning opportunities which advance pupils':

    i. personal and social development;

    ii. communication skills;

    iii. knowledge and understanding of the world;

    iv. physical development;

    v. creative development;

c. use teaching approaches and activities which develop pupils' language and provide the foundations for literacy;

d. use teaching approaches and activities which develop pupils' mathematical understanding and provide the foundations for numeracy;

e. encourage pupils to think and talk about their learning and to develop self-control and independence;

f. encourage pupils to concentrate and persevere in their learning for sustained periods, to listen attentively and to talk about their experiences in small and large groups;

g. use teaching approaches and activities which involve planned adult intervention, which offer opportunities for first-hand experience and co-operation, and which use play and talk as a vehicle for learning;

h. manage, with support from an experienced specialist teacher if necessary, the work of parents and other adults in the classroom to enhance learning opportunities for pupils.

C. MONITORING, ASSESSMENT, RECORDING, REPORTING AND ACCOUNTABILITY

This section details the Standards which all those to be awarded QTS must demonstrate, when assessed, in each subject that they have been trained to teach. For primary non-core, non-specialist subjects, trainees being assessed for QTS must meet the required Standards but with the support, if necessary, of a teacher experienced in the subject concerned.

For all courses, those to be awarded QTS must, when assessed, demonstrate that they:

a. assess how well learning objectives have been achieved and use this assessment to improve specific aspects of teaching;

b. mark and monitor pupils' assigned classwork and homework, providing constructive oral and written feedback, and setting targets for pupils' progress;

c. assess and record each pupil's progress systematically, including through focused observation, questioning, testing and marking, and use these records to:

  i. check that pupils have understood and completed the work set;

  ii. monitor strengths and weaknesses and use the information gained as a basis for purposeful intervention in pupils' learning;

  iii. inform planning;

  iv. check that pupils continue to make demonstrable progress in their acquisition of the knowledge, skills and understanding of the subject;

d. are familiar with the statutory assessment and reporting requirements and know how to prepare and present informative reports to parents;

e. where applicable, understand the expected demands of pupils in relation to each relevant level description or end of key stage description, and, in addition, for those on 11–16 or 18 and 14–19 courses, the demands of the syllabuses and course requirements for GCSE, other KS4 courses, and, where applicable, post-16 courses;

f. where applicable, understand and know how to implement the assessment requirements of current qualifications for pupils aged 14–19;

g. recognise the level at which a pupil is achieving, and assess pupils consistently against attainment targets, where applicable, if necessary with guidance from an experienced teacher;

h. understand and know how national, local, comparative and school data, including National Curriculum test data, where applicable, can be used to set clear targets for pupils' achievement;

i. use different kinds of assessment appropriately for different purposes, including National Curriculum and other standardised tests, and baseline assessment where relevant.

D. OTHER PROFESSIONAL REQUIREMENTS

Primary and secondary

For all courses, those to be awarded QTS should, when assessed, demonstrate that they:

a. have a working knowledge and understanding of:

    i. teachers' professional duties as set out in the current School Teachers' Pay and Conditions document, issued under the School Teachers' Pay and Conditions Act 1991;

    ii. teachers' legal liabilities and responsibilities relating to:

- the Race Relations Act 1976;
- the Sex Discrimination Act 1975;
- Section 7 and Section 8 of the Health and Safety at Work etc. Act 1974;
- teachers' common law duty to ensure that pupils are healthy and safe on school premises and when leading activities off the school site, such as educational visits, school outings or field trips;
- what is reasonable for the purposes of safeguarding or promoting children's welfare (Section 3(5) of the Children Act 1989);
- the role of the education service in protecting children from abuse (currently set out in DfEE Circular 10/95 and the Home Office, Department of Health, DfEE and Welsh Office Guidance *Working Together: A guide to arrangements for inter-agency co-operation for the protection of children from abuse 1991*);
- appropriate physical contact with pupils (currently set out in DfEE Circular 10/95);
- appropriate physical restraint of pupils (Section 4 of the Education Act 1997 and DfEE Circular 9/94);
- detention of pupils on disciplinary grounds (Section 5 of the Education Act 1997);

b. have established, during work in schools, effective working relationships with professional colleagues including, where applicable, associate staff;

c. set a good example to the pupils they teach, through their presentation and their personal and professional conduct;

d. are committed to ensuring that every pupil is given the opportunity to achieve their potential and meet the high expectations set for them;

e. understand the need to take responsibility for their own professional development and to keep up to date with research and developments in pedagogy and in the subjects they teach;

f. understand their professional responsibilities in relation to school policies and practices, including those concerned with pastoral and personal safety matters, including bullying;

g. recognise that learning takes place inside and outside the school context, and understand the need to liaise effectively with parents and other carers and with agencies with responsibility for pupils' education and welfare;

h. are aware of the role and purpose of school governing bodies.

Appendix 2 The NQT Induction Assessment Form (DfEE Circular 5/99)

NQT Induction assessment form for the:

☐ end of first assessment period.   ☐ end of second assessment period.

- This form should be completed by the Headteacher and sent to the Appropriate Body within ten working days of the relevant assessment meeting.
- Where tick boxes appear, please tick the relevant box(es)

9115.1

Full name	
Date of birth	
DfEE reference number of NQT	
National Insurance number of NQT	
Name of school	
DfEE number of school	

Second period assessment: Is this the school that reported at the end of the first period?   ☐ Yes   ☐ No

Name of appropriate body receiving the report

Date of appointment	

NQT's Specialism   ☐ Key stage ▶ *please specify*

☐ Age range ▶ *please specify*

☐ Subject ▶ *please specify*

Does the NQT work: ☐ Part-time? ▶ *please state proportion of a week worked*

☐ Full-time?

Recommendation: ☐ The above named teacher's progress indicates that he/she will be able to meet the requirements for the satisfactory completion of the induction period.

☐ The above named teacher is not making satisfactory progress towards the requirements for the satisfactory completion of the induction period.

Please indicate the kinds of support and monitoring arrangements that have been in place this term.

☐ Observations of the NQT's teaching and provision of feedback.

☐ Discussions between the NQT and the induction tutor to review progress and set targets.

☐ Observations of experienced teachers by the NQT.

☐ An assessment meeting between the NQT and the induction tutor.

☐ Other ▶ *please specify*

- Under the following headings, please give brief details of:
  - the extent to which the NQT **is** meeting the induction standards.
  - in circumstances where the NQT **is not** considered to have made satisfactory progress, details of the following should also be given in the relevant sections:
    - areas of weakness;
    - evidence used to inform the judgement;
    - targets for the coming term; and
    - the support which is planned.
  Reference should be made to the specific standards concerned.
- Please continue on a separate sheet if required.

Planning, teaching and class management.

Monitoring, assessment, recording, reporting and accountability.

Other professional requirements.

Induct1   2   over ▶

Comments by the NQT: I have discussed this report with the induction tutor and/or headteacher and;

☐ have no comments to make.　　　　☐ wish to make the following comments.
▼

School stamp/validation

Signed:

Headteacher
(if different from Induction tutor)　　　Date

Full name *(CAPITALS)*

NQT　　　　　　　　　　　　　Date

Full name *(CAPITALS)*

Induction tutor　　　　　　　　Date

Full name *(CAPITALS)*

Bibliography

Bleach, K. (1999a) 'New Deal for Teachers', *Professional Development Today* **2**(2).

Bleach, K. (1999b) *The Induction and Mentoring of Newly Qualified Teachers*. London: David Fulton Publishers.

Brooks, V. and Sikes, P. (1997) *The Good Mentor Guide*. Buckingham: Open University Press.

Bubb, S. (2000a) 'Caution: Danger Ahead – Newly Qualified Teachers' Induction Standards', *Times Educational Supplement* 14 January.

Bubb, S. (2000b) 'The Spying Game – observing teachers' *Times Educational Supplement* 5 May.

Bubb, S. (2000c) 'Stand up for your rights – advice for newly qualified teachers' *Times Educational Supplement* 5 May.

Bubb, S. (2000d) 'How and when to lay down the law' *Times Educational Supplement* 5 May.

Bullough, R. V. (1989) *First-Year Teacher – a case study*. New York: Teachers College Press.

DfEE (1998a) *Teaching: High Status, High Standards*. Circular 4/98. London: DfEE.

DfEE (1998b) *Induction for Newly Qualified Teachers. A Consultation Document*. London: DfEE.

DfEE (1998c) *School Teachers' Pay and Conditions of Employment 1998*. Circular 9/98. London: DfEE.

DfEE (1999) *The Induction Period for Newly Qualified Teachers*. Circular 5/99. London: DfEE.

Earley, P. and Kinder, K. (1994) *Initiation Rights – Effective Induction Practices for New Teachers*. Slough: NFER.

Eraut, M. (1994) *Developing Professional Knowledge and Competence*. London: Falmer Press.

Ghaye, A. and Ghaye, K. (1998) *Teaching and Learning through Critical Reflective Practice*. London: David Fulton Publishers.

Hagger, H. and McIntyre, D. (1994) *Mentoring in Secondary Schools. Reading 8: Learning Through Analysing Practice*. Milton Keynes: Open University.

Hagger, H., Burn, K. and McIntyre, D. (1993) *The School Mentor Handbook*. London: Kogan Page.

Hayes, D. (2000) *The Handbook for Newly Qualified Teachers – Meeting the Standards in Primary and Middle Schools*. London: David Fulton Publishers.

Heilbron, R. and Jones, C. (eds) (1997) *New Teachers in an Urban Comprehensive School*. Stoke: Trentham Books.

HMI (1988) *The New Teacher in School*. London: HMSO.

Hustler, D. and McIntyre, D. (eds) (1996) *Developing Competent Teachers*. London: David Fulton Publishers.

James Committee (1972) *Teacher Education and Training*. London: HMSO.

McIntyre, D. and Hagger, H. (1996) *Mentors in Schools. Developing the Profession of Teaching*. London: David Fulton Publishers.

Malderez, A. and Bodoczky, C. (1999) *Mentor Courses – a resource book for trainers*. Cambridge: Cambridge University Press.

Maynard, T. and Furlong, J. (1993) 'Learning to teach and models of mentoring', in Kerry, T. and Shelton Mayes, (eds) (1995) A. *Issues in Mentoring*. London: Routledge/Open University.

Montgomery, D. (1999) *Positive Teacher Appraisal Through Classroom Observation*. London: David Fulton Publishers.

Moyles, J., Suschitsky, W. and Chapman, L. (1999) 'Mentoring in Primary Schools: ethos, structures and workload', *Journal of In-service Education* **25**(1).

OFSTED (1999) *Handbook for Inspecting Primary and Nursery Schools*. London: The Stationery Office.

Richards, C. (2000) 'You don't have to be a genius, but . . .' Letter 7 January 2000, *TES*.

TTA (1999a) *Career Entry Profile*. London: TTA.

TTA (1999b) *Supporting Induction for Newly Qualified Teachers. Part 1: Overview*. London: TTA.

TTA (1999c) *Supporting Induction for Newly Qualified Teachers. Part 2: Support and Monitoring of the Newly Qualified Teacher*. London: TTA.

TTA (1999d) *Supporting Induction for Newly Qualified Teachers. Part 3: Assessment of the Newly Qualified Teacher*. London: TTA.

TTA (1999e) *Supporting Induction for Newly Qualified Teachers. Part 4: Quality Assurance of the Induction Arrangements*. London: TTA.

Vonk, J. (1993) 'Mentoring beginning teachers: mentor knowledge and skills', *Mentoring* **1**(1), 31–41.

Williams, A. and Prestage, S. (2000) *Still in at the deep end? Developing strategies for the induction of new teachers*. London: Association of Teachers and Lecturers.

Winnacott, D. W. (1971) *Playing and Reality*. London: Tavistock.

Woods, P. and Jeffreys, B. (1996) *Teachable Moments. The Art of Teaching in Primary Schools*. Buckingham: Open University Press.

Wu, J. (1998) 'School Work Environment and its Impact on the Professional Competence of Newly Qualified Teachers', *Journal of In-service Education* **24**(2).

Yeomans, R. and Sampson, J. (eds) (1994) *Mentorship in the Primary School*. London: Falmer Press.

Index

www.ingramcontent.com/pod-product-compliance
Ingram Content Group UK Ltd.
Pitfield, Milton Keynes, MK11 3LW, UK
UKHW050013280225
455677UK00025B/798